Beechcraft
Staggerwing

The
Flying Classics

SERIES

Other Books in the Flying Classics Series

Beechcraft Staggerwing

Peter Berry

TAB BOOKS
Blue Ridge Summit, PA

FIRST EDITION
FIRST PRINTING

Copyright 1990 by **TAB BOOKS**
Printed in the United States of America

Library of Congress Cataloging − in − Publication Data

Berry, Peter.
    Beechcraft staggerwing / by Peter Berry.
      p.   cm.
    Includes bibliographical references.
    ISBN 0-8306-8410-7 :
    1. Beechcraft (Airplanes) 1. Title.
TL686.B36B47 1990
629.133'343—dc20   89-48459
                                          CIP

TAB BOOKS offers software for sale. For information and a catalog, please contact
TAB Software Department, Blue Ridge Summit, PA 17294-0850.

Questions regarding the content of this book should be addressed to:

    Reader Inquiry Branch
    TAB BOOKS
    Blue Ridge Summit, PA 17294-0214

Acquisitions Editor: Jeff Worsinger
Technical Editor: Steven H. Mesner
Production: Katherine Brown
Series Design: Jaclyn J. Boone

Frontcover: Formatting on the camera of Roger Bunce, this Model G175 was delivered
September 21, 1946, to W.S. Carpenter III, Wilmington, DE. Following several owners it
was rebuilt and N99DV is now proudly owned by E.D. Vincent, Montecito, CA.

Contents

Foreword

When Walter Beech and Ted Wells brought their Model 17 to production in 1934, they little realized the design would begin a long line of trend-setting business aircraft continued by the Beech Aircraft Corporation to this day.

This innovative, negative-stagger, four-to-five seat biplane with retractable undercarriage, powered by a variety of engines, proved to be a most saleable design. By 1942, 353 Model 17s had been sold in North and South America, Europe, India, Japan, South Africa, the Philippines, Australia, and New Zealand. Military versions served the United States Navy and Air Corps and the armed forces of Finland, China, Brazil, Honduras, Argentina, Uruguay, and Honduras. Lend-Lease saw further deliveries to the British Royal Navy and Royal Air Force, China, Brazil and Bolivia.

In postwar years, surviving Staggerwings declined until the mid-1960s, when the Staggerwing Club and Museum Foundation provided the catalyst for the owner-pilot and aircraft restorer to return to service an increasing number of Beechcraft Model 17s—to the delight of a growing number of enthusiastic supporters of the classic biplane design.

John L. Parish, President
Staggerwing Museum Foundation, Inc.
P.O. Box 550, Tullahoma, TN 37388

Acknowledgments

Among the files and memorabilia and in the hearts of many aviation people is a place for the Beechcraft Model 17 negative-stagger biplane. One of the true classic biplanes, it was designed by Ted Wells and built by Walter Beech in the Golden Age of flying, the 1930s.

My file on this Beechcraft goes back to a copy of *The Aeroplane* dated July 7, 1944, in which the cartoonist "Wren" sketched the wartime UC-43 military variant as the 167th "Oddentification," a series used to aid the wartime Allies in their aircraft recognition. The drawing is reproduced on the facing page and was copied by John Bagley from the Science Museum Archive, London, and is reproduced courtesy of the *Aeroplane Monthly*.

Additions to the file were made through the years until 1963, when Robert T. Smith wrote me seeking information on the many single-engined Beechcrafts exported to Europe and elsewhere. In addition to researching this data and collecting photographs for his manuscript, I wrote to the Foreign Office in London, asking for the address of Sir Harold L. Farquhar. In 1935, Farquhar flew the 50th production Model 17 from Mexico to London, via the United States, Canada, Siberia, China, India, the Middle East, and across the Mediterranean to England. In due course, his son Adrian found and lent me the hand-written diary of the flight, a summary of which is found in Chapter 6.

A visit to aviation historian Bill Larkins in 1977 drew my attention to the Media Newsletter of the Staggerwing Museum Foundation, which led to my membership in that organization and visits to the Foundation's facility at Tullahoma, Tennessee. Here I found the archives of the Beechcraft Model 17 and a wealth of later material that, with the approval of Foundation President John L. Parish, is published here for the first time. Acknowledgment is made to George and Mattie Schulz for their patience during my research, to the Museum Media and Club newsletters, and to the past research notes of Ed Phillips, George York, Tom Lempicke, Glenn McNabb, Hub Johnson, and "Dub" Yarbrough.

Staggerwing owner Bill Halverson kindly gave his permission to use the Model G175S pilot checklist found in Appendix G.

Research of this kind is never possible without the kind assistance of many aviation names. Acknowledgment is duly given to the time and efforts of William T. Larkins for his photographs and data on the early U.S. Navy versions of the Beechcraft and the prewar CAA civil aircraft registers of owners. John A. Whittle transcribed many of the U.S. Navy and Army Air Force record cards for me, and John M. Davis resolved many of the subsequent civil identities.

Vic Seely, Curator of the Museum of Flight, Seattle, Washington, forwarded many photographs from their new facility, and Peter M. Bowers searched his files for photographs and also kindly read the manuscript proof. Aviation photographers Douglas D. Olson, Stan Staples, Arthur Pearcy, Al Hansen, and Bill Landers searched their photo collections for pictures I needed, and Staggerwing Foundation photographer Roger Bunce selected several of his fine photographs for the cover and text. Ruth Warden provided a color photo of the Planes of Fame East Staggerwing. Col. T. Petras, USMC, and Wing Commander David Bennett, RAF, offered photographs of their flying activities with military Beechcraft 17s. The Fleet Air Arm Museum approved the printing of the Royal Navy Traveller, and Pat Zerbe approved the use of the Beech Aircraft Corporation factory photographs, printed from the negative files held by Brian Nicholas at the National Air and Space Museum, Washington, D.C. He also found photographs from the Smithsonian Collection.

First-hand experiences of flying the early fixed and retractable-gear Beechcraft biplanes were given to me by veteran Beechcraft pilot Eddie Ross. Museum Foundation President John L. Parish gave my wife Jenny and me the opportunity to fly in his "Big Red" Model G17S at Tullahoma in October 1988.

Reference has been made to many of the Air-Britain (Historian) publications dating from 1948, in particular the issues of *Archive* for 1984–85, edited by David Partington. Bill Burkinshaw of Argus Specialist Publications gave his approval to reproduce *The Aeromodeller* drawings of the Models D and G17S. A bibliography of further reading on the Beechcraft Model 17 is contained in an appendix.

Royalties from the sale of this book have been assigned by me to the Staggerwing Museum Foundation, Inc., to continue the restoration, upkeep, and display of the Beechcraft Model 17 Staggerwing.

Introduction

When pilots, enthusiasts, and the public made their way to the All-American Air Maneuvers at Miami, Florida, in January 1933, they looked—as we all do today—for the skill and daring of the air racing and airshow pilots, and to ask each other "what's new?" in aircraft design. There was a new design on the Miami airport apron that year, the Beechcraft Model 17, first flown only weeks before the event and now entered in the Texaco Trophy Race.

Walter Beech and his air race pilot, Eric H. Woods, were both quietly confident of a good showing in the race, as the prototype biplane had recorded a speed of just over 200 mph in tests at the factory in Wichita, Kansas. During the run-up to the final race days, Karl E. Voelter piloted the new Beechcraft prototype around the race circuit. The enthusiasm of the crowd of spectators was raised by the airshow commentator: "Just look at that negative-staggerwing go!", he cried, as the speeding Beechcraft banked steeply round the last pylon, and with its Wright Whirlwind engine roaring, sped past in front of the crowd.

The forthcoming success for Walter Beech in the Texaco Trophy Race served notice that this new aircraft manufacturing company was going to produce high-performance aircraft in the future and a new name was to be added to classic aircraft design: the Staggerwing.

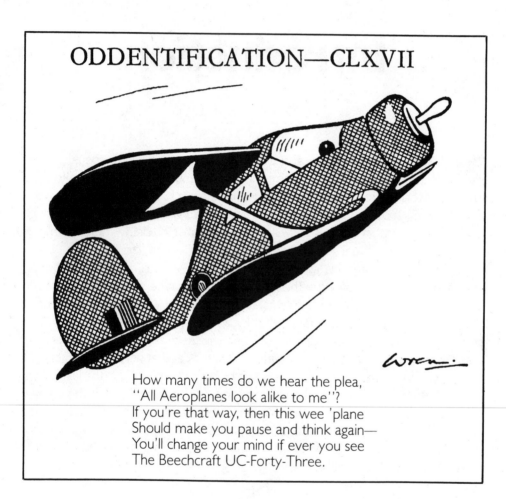

ODDENTIFICATION—CLXVII

How many times do we hear the plea,
"All Aeroplanes look alike to me"?
If you're that way, then this wee 'plane
Should make you pause and think again—
You'll change your mind if ever you see
The Beechcraft UC-Forty-Three.

About the author

Peter Berry is a member of and contributor to the Journals of the Royal Aeronautical Society, American Aviation Historical Society and Air-Britain Historians. He served 40 years in the air traffic control towers at the Royal Aircraft Establishments at Farnborough and Bedford and at the Scottish Airways and Shanwick Oceanic Control Centres at Prestwick, Scotland, until his retirement in 1987. His last five years of service was to lead the ATC Applications Team in introducing computers to Oceanic Air Traffic Control. This is Peter's first title for TAB Books.

I-I Walter Herschel Beech (1891–1950). He served with Laird, Swallow, Travel Air, and Curtiss-Wright before forming the Beech Aircraft Company in 1932.

1

The Birth of Beechcraft

Walter Herschel Beech was a farmer's son, born January 30, 1891, in Pulaski, Tennessee (Fig. 1-1). Educated in local grammar and night schools, his natural interest in things mechanical led him to become a sales engineer for the White Company, a truck manufacturer, and he toured Europe for two years as their representative. After acquiring an early Curtiss pusher airplane, Beech made his first flight on July 11, 1914. Three years later he enlisted in the U.S. Army Signal Corps and was sent to Rich Field, Waco, Texas, where, as a head sergeant, he was put in charge of motor transport (including airplanes). During this time he may have managed some part-time flying instruction at the base.

His later career with Laird, Swallow, Travel Air, and Curtiss-Wright broadened Beech's aeronautical experience and showed his demand for blunt, forthright decision and unrelenting standards to achieve the very best in aircraft design, production and performance. Before 1927, he was General Manager of Travel Air and held posts in the Aeronautical Chamber of Commerce of America, Kansas State Committee, and the Engineering Standards, Rules, and Regulation Committee.

Following his discharge from the Army in 1920, Walter Beech renewed a friendship with W.H. "Pete" Hill, who operated the Williams-Hill Airplane Company in Kansas City, Kansas. He spent his days flying a war-surplus Curtiss Jenny for air charters, and giving joyrides, aerial advertising and "barnstorming" demonstrations at airshows around the country.

EM Laird Airplane Company

After a disastrous fire at the Williams-Hill facility in April 1921, Walter Beech left and the following month was hired by financier Jacob Melvin "Jake" Moellendick as a test and demonstration pilot and general "handyman" for the E.M. Laird Airplane Company of Wichita, Kansas. Here he joined Lloyd Carlton Stearman, who was busy building all-wood wings and fuselages for the three-place Laird Swallow biplane (Fig. 1-2). William "Bill" Snook managed the shop floor. Walter Beech was able to develop his skills as a demonstration and air race pilot, mechanic, and friendly salesperson—qualities he later put to good use when he managed his own company.

Swallow Airplane Manufacturing Company

Following a disagreement in policy with Moellendick, designer "Matty" Laird left in January 1924 and the renamed Swallow Airplane Manufacturing Company continued, with Walter Beech in charge of flying activities and Lloyd Stearman as chief designer/engineer. Two months later, design work was completed and production began of the New Swallow which now had a divided-axle landing gear, a close-cowled engine, and a belly radiator (Fig. 1-3). Walter Beech flew one of the new biplanes to victory in the On-to-Detroit Cross-Country Classic and the July Admiral Fullman Derby, and won the efficiency contest organized by the Aviation Town and Country Club of Detroit.

The Travel Air years

Late in 1924, Stearman, Snook, and Beech left the Swallow Company, having unsuccessfully argued with Moellendick to introduce a welded-steel fuselage update to the all-wood Swallow design. Early aviator Clyde Vernon Cessna was invited by Beech and Stearman to form a new company with financial backing from Walter P. Innes Jr. Incorporated in February 1925, the Travel Air Manufacturing Company had premises at 471 West First Street in Wichita. The combined skills of these three now-ledgendary names in aviation resulted in the completion of the metal-framed Travel Air biplane, using the close-cowled OX-5 and belly radiator from the New Swallow but with an improved landing gear (Fig. 1-4). Walter Beech soon sealed the success of the design at the Tulsa Air Meet. He went on to score top marks flying a Model B6 in the 1925 Ford Reliability Tour and, with Brice Goldsborough navigating the Model BW, won the 2,585-mile 1926 Tour, scoring most points based on several parameters tied to performance over the route.

Two innovations proven in the 1926 Tour were wheel brakes for shorter landing runs and ground maneuvering, and, to ensure efficient operation in flight, a complete set of flight, navigation and engine instruments. These were installed in the Travel Air by the Pioneer Instrument Company.

Walter Beech hired Clarence E. Clark as chief test pilot for Travel Air and he flew a Model BH in the 1926 Ford Reliability Tour. During his five years with the company, Clarence Clark test-flew more than 700 production Travel Airs, including the first Model 6000 monoplane and four of the five Model R "Mystery Ships."

1-2 The Laird Swallow three-place biplane—essentially a "cleaned-up" Curtiss Jenny powered by the same 90-hp Curtiss OX-5 eight-cylinder V engine.

1-3 The "New Swallow" shows the closely-cowled Curtiss OX-5 engine, divided axle landing gear, and belly radiator—great advances for 1924.

The Birth of Beechcraft   **3**

Walter Beech was also instrumental in giving a young Miss Louise Mc-Phetridge the chance to join the Pacific Coast Travel Air Distributor, D.C. Warren, learn the aviation business, and also learn to fly. She was to return this favor in later years.

In 1926, Travel Air was moved to larger premises, first behind the Broadview Hotel and then to a building at 535 West Douglas Avenue, Wichita. As company business expanded, a bookkeeper-office manager was hired in the attractive form of Miss Olive Ann Mellor, who efficiently took care of the administration. She was later to marry Walter Beech, and in 1950, as the "First Lady of Aviation," she became President of the Beech Aircraft Corporation following Walter's death.

Early in 1927, Walter Beech was shown a high-wing cabin monoplane design that Clyde Cessna had been building in his spare time. Cessna had a hard time overcoming Beech's resistance to monoplane designs, but with interest warming to cabin monoplanes and air mail contracts to be won, the new six-place, Wright Whirlwind-powered Model 5000 was added to the Travel Air range. With an order for eight of the new Model from National Air Transport, the high-wing design demonstrated its performance with the first civilian flight to Hawaii from California in July 1927, the prototype being flown by Ernest L. Smith and Emory Bronte. (This occurred before pineapple king James Dole offered a $25,000 prize for a similar Pacific crossing. Arthur C. Goebel and Lt. William V. Davis, USN, went on to win this prize with a successful Pacific crossing in the Travel Air 5000 *Woolaroc* the following month.)

In June 1927, Travel Air moved to a new factory at East Central, Wichita, alongside the new airport, the present home of the Beech Aircraft Corporation. Walter Beech, now President of a reorganized Travel Air Company, replaced Stearman and Cessna (who had left to develop their own sporting biplane and

1-4 Walter Beech piloting the first Travel Air biplane completed in 1924. Powered by a 90-hp Curtiss OX-5 engine, this protoype was the forerunner of more than a thousand Travel Airs built through 1931.

cantilever monoplane designs); Herb Rawdon and Walter Burnham would continue engineering development of the Travel Air line. Purchasing agent and chief inspector was Walter's brother, R.K. Beech, engineering pilot was Ted A. Wells, Wichita capitalist was C.G. Yankey, and New York broker and financial adviser was T.D. Neelands. This team was later to form the heart of Beech's own company.

Rawdon and Burham proposed a monoplane racing design, the Model R, for the 1929 National Air Races at Cleveland. At earlier Race meetings, the U.S. Army and Navy military aircraft had always won the speed prizes and Walter Beech was intrigued with the proposal to build a civilian low-wing monoplane. Powered by a specially prepared 400-hp Wright R-975 Whirlwind engine housed in the new NACA cowl and featuring steamlined wheel pants, this craft would exceed the performance of the military designs (Fig. 1-5).

Work was commenced and in some ten weeks the first of the Model R racers was completed, soon showing its paces. A second Model R was completed in time for the races. Because the design was built with no publicity and kept under wraps until the start of the race, the press soon dubbed the machine the "Mystery Ship." Piloted by Travel Air dealer Douglas D. Davis, the Chevrolair-powered machine captured the Experimental Ship Race and the Wright Whirlwind-powered Model R (R614K) (Fig. 1-6) beat the military Curtiss P-3A and F6C-6 Hawks in the 50-mile Free-for-All Race with an average speed of 194.96 mph—even though Davis had to circle one plyon twice to ensure he hadn't missed it!

Three further Model R machines were built—one for Texaco, one for Shell Oil, and one for the Italian government. They were flown by such noted pilots as Dale Jackson, J.H. "Jimmy" Doolittle, Walter Hunter, and Florence Lowe "Pancho" Barnes, adding new honors to this revolutionary design. The Chief Pilot of the Texas Company, Captain Frank Hawks, established more than 200 new speed records in America and Europe, flying the Model R *Texaco 13*. The Model R might have influenced the development of military aircraft in several countries, including Italy, which bought the final Model R completed. Some design details can also be seen in the high-speed Staggerwing biplane later developed by Ted Wells, the stress analysist and designer working with Herb Rawdon.

Louise McPhetridge married ex-Army pilot and San Francisco-based aircraft manufacturer Herbert von Thaden in June 1928. She was the fourth American woman to earn an Air Transport Licence and added further laurels to the Travel Air designs by setting the first officially recorded Women's Altitude Record on December 7, 1928, coaxing a 180-hp Hispano-Suiza-powered Travel Air 3000 to an altitude of 20,260 feet. Flying Travel Air 3000 (5426), Louise went on to set a Women's solo non-refuelled endurance record of 22:03:12 hours on March

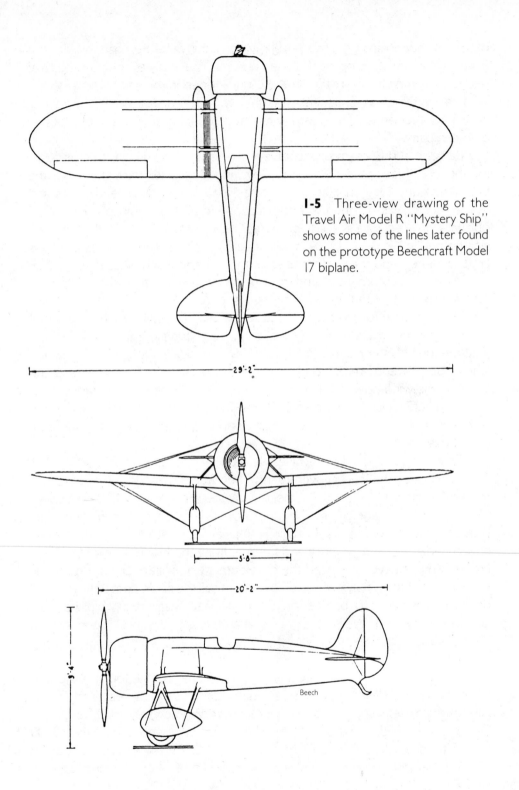

1-5 Three-view drawing of the Travel Air Model R "Mystery Ship" shows some of the lines later found on the prototype Beechcraft Model 17 biplane.

29'-2"

5'-8"

20'-2"

9'-4"

Beech

16–17, 1929. With speed wings fitted to a Travel Air, she set a Women's world speed record of 156 mph at Oakland on April 13, 1929. In August, this time flying a specially built blue and gold 220-hp Wright J-5 Whirlwind-powered Travel Air D-4000 with speed wings (NR671H), she took first place in the National Women's Santa Monica–Cleveland Air Derby with a time of 20:02:02 hours and an average speed of 135.97 mph (Fig. 1-7). This was no mean achievement, as she was flying against such noted competition as "Pancho" Barnes, Blanche Noyes, Amelia Earhart, Ruth Nichols, Thea Rasche, Ruth Elder, and Mae Haizlip.

Curtiss-Wright takeover

By July 1929, Travel Air was producing a range of three cabin monoplanes and nine open biplane designs. Under the able direction of Walter Beech, they had sold some 949 aircraft since 1925, with production peaking at 25 aircraft a week. However, to gain new funds to finance this expansion, controlling interest in the company was sold to the newly formed Curtiss-Wright Corporation, with Walter Beech serving as Vice-President of Sales as well as President of the Airplane Division in Wichita.

Beech

1-6 The first Travel Air Model R (R614K) powered by a 420-hp Wright R-975 Whirlwind engine. Pilot Douglas H. Davis flew this "Mystery Ship" to first place in the 1929 Thompson Trophy Race at Cleveland at an average 194.96 mph.

Curtiss-Wright introduced their own system of designating models following the takeover, commencing with CW-12 and reaching CW-16 when Walter Beech left the Company.

Following the stock market crash of 1929, production of Travel Air models declined. In 1931, the Wichita factory was closed and production was transfered to the Curtiss-Wright facility at Robertson, St. Louis, Missouri. More than 1,300 Travel Air aircraft had been built as such, plus a few new "C-W" models developed after the Curtiss takeover.

Meanwhile, engineer Ted Wells had been considering a new layout for a high-speed cabin biplane with a difference—negative wing stagger. When Curtiss-Wright executives showed no interest in the project, the design was put to one side.

1-7 Louise Thaden and the Travel Air D-4000 (NR671H) in which she won the 129 National Women's Santa Monica–Cleveland Air Derby in 20 hours, 20 minutes and 2 seconds. Restoration of this Travel Air by W.C. "Dub" Yarborough is scheduled for 1989.

Fixed-gear
Model 17

Becoming increasingly frustrated with his journeyings to St. Louis to oversee aircraft production, and to New York for meetings of the board, Walter Beech and his wife Ann decided to move back to Wichita and start their own aircraft company. Beech resigned his positions with Curtiss-Wright in late 1931 and began to lay plans for the manufacture of a revolutionary biplane design.

Model 17 Design

Walter Beech put engineer Ted Wells to work completing the design of the high-speed biplane project that Curtiss-Wright had rejected. The design was expected to appeal to the business executive and sports flier. Showing some of the lines of the famed Travel Air "Mystery Ship," a four-to-five-seat cabin biplane emerged from the drawing board offering comfort and performance with compact dimensions and good control throughout the speed range (Fig. 2-1). A unique feature was the *negative-stagger wing* layout; that is, the upper wing was set behind the lower one, the opposite arrangement to contemporary biplanes. Wind tunnel tests of this setting showed outstanding stall and recovery characteristics, good visibility for the pilot, and a natural location for a later development, retractable landing gear (Fig. 2-2). There was also a structural advantage: The duplicated set of flying wires were attached to the upper front spar only at the outer strut fittings, and then passed through the lower wing to the landing gear. The landing wires, also attached to the upper wing only, picked up points on both spars of the lower wing, thus forming a very deep and rigid truss system.

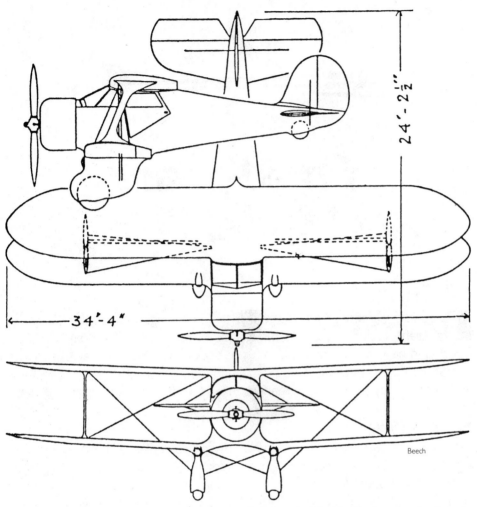

24'-2½"

34'-4"

Beech

2-1 Three-view drawing of the prototype Beechcraft Model 17, showing the heavily trousered narrow-track landing gear and negative-stagger wing arrangement.

There were no wing landing flaps on the first two prototypes. As an aid to deceleration and to increase rudder effectiveness at slow speeds for landing, rudder surfaces split along the centerline were engineered, preceding the Space Shuttle arrangement by some 50 years! These were activated by a lever in the cockpit.

A full-scale working mockup was built in the old Cessna hangar with the assistance of Theodore Joseph Cochrane, a construction mechanic from the Travel Air factory. The mockup included stub wings, controls, and a complete molded glass windshield. This windshield was the first to be manufactured by the Pittsburgh Plate Glass Company for either the auto or aircraft industries.

Theodore Cochrane's brother William was foreman for the primary assembly of the prototype Beechcraft. Its construction materials followed the experience gained from the production of earlier Travel Air and Curtiss-Wright designs—a conventional steel tubing fuselage with wood and metal formers and wood stringers. The 34′4″ span wings used the Navy N-9 airfoil section and were made up with steel-tube truss spars with faired I struts, streamlined flying and landing wires, and metal leading edges. The tail unit was of metal tubing with wire-braced horizontal tail surfaces. Longitudinal trim was effected by a motorized jack on the stabilizer. The forward fuselage to aft of the left and right entry doors was metal-covered. The rear fuselage, wings, and tail unit were fabric-covered. A 175-pound capacity baggage compartment was located aft of the cabin. The coloring of the prototype was Insignia Red with Dark Maroon striping and registration numbers.

The main wheels of the landing gear were faired and electrically retracted into pants, leaving about six inches of tire exposed. The fixed tailwheel was faired into the rear fuselage. The two fuel tanks, totalling 145 gallons, were

2-2 The original wind tunnel test model of the Beechcraft negative-stagger biplane, donated by Sol Bachos, Wichita, and on display at the Staggerwing Museum Foundation, Tullahoma, Tennessee.

located fore and aft under the passenger cabin. The 420-hp Wright R-975-E2 Whirlwind nine-cylinder radial engine was enclosed in a NACA-type cowl and fitted with a Lycoming-Smith controllable propeller.

The first Staggerwings

The new Beechcraft Model 17 (499N), so designated to follow the previous Curtiss-Wright Model 16, was rolled out of the factory and following ground handling tests, "Pete" Hill recorded in his logbook the first flight on November 5, 1932, seven months after design work began. Design estimates were soon proven, and on November 11th, a speed of 201.2 mph was recorded over an officially observed course. A comfortable cruise speed of 180 mph and a non-stop range of 1,000 miles were also achieved. Rate of climb was 1,600 fpm, ceiling over 20,000 feet, and the landing speed just 60 mph—a remarkable performance range for the time (Fig. 2-3).

Following exhaustive testing and demonstration flights to a wide range of pilots, Approved Type Certificate Number A-496 was awarded to the Model 17R on December 20, 1932. Seeking an early sale, the first of the panted-gear Beechcrafts (NC499N) was entered for the 1933 Miami Air Races. The second Model 17R (NC58Y), however, was to be the first sale of the Beechcraft; this was completed and delivered in July 1933 to the oil well-drilling Loffland Brothers in Tulsa, Oklahoma (Fig. 2-4). The prototype was not sold until May of the following year, when the Ethyl Corporation took delivery.

Loffland company pilot Eddie Ross recalls that Ted Wells had set the incidence of the wings at 2 degrees above the stalling attitude when on the ground.

2-3 Walter Beech with the prototype Model 17R. Note the heavily trousered narrow track landing gear and the cleanly cowled Wright R-975 Whirlwind engine.

William N. Fleming

2-4 Loffland Brothers pilot Eddie Ross with the second Model 17R (NC58Y) at Rita Santa, Texas. It was delivered in July 1933 and flown for two years until traded in for a B17E, then dismantled at the factory. Note the narrow track gear, cowl scoops, and glossy finish.

Douglas D. Olson

2-5 The first Model A17F (NC12583) with huge 690-hp Wright R-1820 Cyclone engine. Maximum and cruise speeds of this model were well ahead of contemporary fighter aircraft.

This led to interesting takeoff and landing characteristics, which had to be countered by getting the tail up early for takeoff and keeping the tail high for landing. When Eddie asked Ted Wells the reason for this setting, Wells replied, " 'Cause we get strong winds in Kansas and I didn't want it to blow away!''

Two more panted-gear Beechcrafts, designated A-17F, were built in 1934–5 (NC12583 and NC12569), and were powered by 690 to 710-hp Wright R-1820 Cyclone engines. The performance of these models, with top and cruise speeds of 225 and 215 mph, was well ahead of military fighter aircraft of the

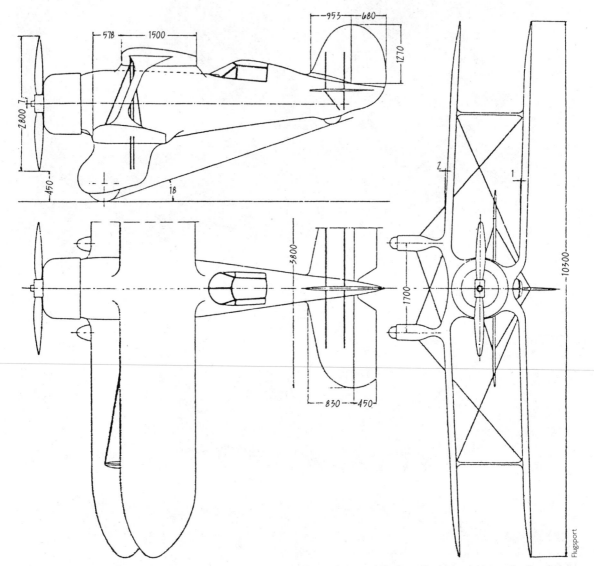

2-6 Three-view of the single-seat military Model A17J project, with the pilot's cockpit well aft of the negative-staggered wings. Wing drawings for this version have been preserved.

day (Fig. 2-5). These had a wider track landing gear, swivelling tailwheel, and decelerator flaps on the underside of the upper wing replacing the split rudder on the first Beechcraft. The rudder and elevators were aerodynamically balanced and an elevator tab was provided for trim in place of the adjustable tailplane. An interesting feature was rear seat shock absorbers, which were fitted to reduce passenger fatique on long flights.

Design work was also begun on a single-seat military version, the Model 17J (Fig. 2-6). Powered by a 715-hp Wright Cyclone, its pilot's cockpit was located aft of the wing trailing edge and a new upper gull-wing arrangement allowed the pilot to see forward over the wing. The wing drawings for this model have been preserved in the Staggerwing Museum Foundation.

3

Variants and production

With the Depression affecting the sale of powerful, fast executive aircraft, Walter Beech agreed with Ted Wells to scale down the dimensions, power, and performance of the Model 17 prototypes. The Model B17 introduced retractable undercarriage and a modified Clark CYH wing section to the Beechcraft. The plan was to share the business market with similarly powered Waco and Stinson designs.

Model B17L prototype

The various Models of the Beechcraft 17 were identified, following the two prototypes, by a designation system using the Model 17 number prefixed by a series letter and suffixed by an engine letter. Thus, the first production Model 17 was the B17L (NC270Y), which was powered by the recently introduced 225-hp Jacobs L-4 seven-cylinder radial engine turning a Hartzell wooden fixed-pitch propeller. It was rolled out of the factory painted in a dark red (maroon) color scheme with the fuselage and tail scallops painted black and was flown February 2, 1934 (Fig. 3-1). The Model B17L was displayed at the 1935 Detroit Air Show, with a price tag of $8,000, to the great interest of dealers and pilots alike.

Detail changes from the early fixed-gear Beechcrafts were the reduced 32-foot span of the wings (now made with wooden spars) and the location of the fuel tanks, one in each upper wing root, totalling 50 gallons. An option was the fitting of tanks in the lower wing roots and one fuselage tank for a total of 120 gallons. Deceleration flaps replaced the split rudder; these were fitted to the lower wings ahead of the ailerons and were operated by a lever in the cockpit (Fig. 3-2). These devices increased the drag, steepened the approach, and added somewhat to aileron effectiveness, much like the effect of the turbulator strips used on today's aircraft. An elevator tab simplified longitudinal trim and a single upper and lower strut braced the tailplane, replacing the wire brace of the fixed-gear models.

"Long" main undercarriage legs (Fig. 3-3) retracted neatly inwards into the lower wing. The cabin entry door was on the left side of the fuselage; an additional right hand door was optional. A further option was the fitting of Irvin or Switlik parachutes into the upholstery of specially designed seats. Standard instruments included a Kollsman airspeed indicator and altimeter, Pioneer oil pressure, tachometer, and oil temperature gauges, compass, and a standard automobile-type ammeter.

A contemporary feature was the mechanical "Johnson bar" differential wheelbrake system, still retained on some early aircraft. The "bar" was a lever in the cockpit (Fig. 3-4) that was pulled on against a ratchet and provided braking on both wheels when the rudder pedal was centralized and differentially when either rudder pedal was depressed.

During the spring and summer of 1934, the first Model B17L (NC270Y) was flight-tested to obtain the Civil Aeronautics Board Approved Type Certificate and ATC Number A-560 was awarded December 4, 1934. This model was retained for a while by Beech as the company demonstration aircraft and it was

3-1 Prototype of the Model B17L (NC270Y) showing the "long" retractable landing gear and cleanly cowled 255-hp Jacobs L-4 engine. Museum of Flight

3-2 Decelerator flaps shown open on the undersurface of the lower wings ahead of the ailerons on a Model B17L (NC15485). The decelerators were moved to the underside of the upper wing on the Models B17E/R and C17E/R, replaced by plain flaps on the lower wings of the Models D17 through G17.

3-3 The "long" main landing gear legs only appeared on the Model B-17L and B-17B variants.

flown by many famous pilots before being sold to Mrs. Charlotte Frye in February 1935. It had an unusual Haywood engine starter that operated on compressed air, similar to very early automobiles. This system was also used to retract the undercarriage—which it did with great gusto, frequently startling pilots as it snapped the wheels up into the underside of the fuselage. After factory serial #36, the Beechcraft undercarriage retraction system was changed to an electric motor with manual reversion.

17 production

With orders for the new Model 17 at last beginning to come in, Walter Beech moved production back to the former Travel Air facility at East Central in April 1934, which he leased from Curtiss-Wright (Fig. 3-5).

3-4 Cockpit of the B17L (NC15400) showing the single throw-over control wheel. The handle in the center panel is for gear up/down latches. The left-hand lever is used to operate the decelerator flaps. The right-hand lever is the dreaded "Johnson Bar" differential wheel brake system.

The production models of the four/five-seat Beechcraft design were offered with a variety of engine and airframe improvements over the next few years. They were also Certificated for use on floats and skis. These models are summarized in the following sections.

B17 production series

Production Model B17L Beechcrafts were similar to the prototype, but the tailplane had an additional lower strut (Fig. 3-6). The sole 285-hp Jacobs L-5-powered B-17B Model (NC14408) was delivered to the Olson Drilling Company in December 1934. It was later sold and registered to F & W Martin and Co. of Tulsa, Oklahoma, who converted it to a B17L with the installation of the 225-hp Jacobs L-4. It was returned to the factory for revised weight and balance checks and certificated as a four-place Beechcraft.

In 1935, the first of the 285-hp Wright R-760 seven-cylinder Whirlwind-powered B-17E models (NC12593) showed several changes to the airframe (Fig. 3-7). The drag flaps were moved to the undersurface of the upper wings, the main undercarriage legs were shortened to improve the takeoff and landing characteristics, and a different wingtip shape reduced the wing area. Standard fuel was carried in two under-floor fuselage tanks totalling 70 gallons, but up to four wing tanks could be fitted for a total of 170 gallons. A metal fixed-pitch Curtiss-Reed or controllable Hamilton-Standard propeller could be fitted.

With the U.S. economy slowly improving and markets moving ahead, production continued through 1936. At the request of Eddie Ross, pilot for the Loffland Drilling Company, their B17E (NC14413) was uprated by the installation of the 420-hp Wright R-975 nine-cylinder engine, so introducing the Model B17R (Fig. 3-8).

Smithsonian/Beech

3-5 Walter Beech with an early Model B17L (NC12598).

3-6 Tail unit of the production Model B17L (NC15485) showing the single upper and twin lower struts used on production B17, C17, E17 and F17 models.

3-7 The Model B17E (NC12593) was powered by the Wright R-760 engine and showed the neater "sit" on the ground with its "short" main landing gear. This improved the takeoff and landing characteristics, but the Staggerwing always demands close attention close to the ground.

The B17R was the first model to be fitted with "blind-flying" instruments, a Pioneer turn-and-bank and rate of climb indicators. Additional engine instruments included cylinder head temperature, fuel and manifold pressure, and fuel contents gauges and a clock.

With 35 employees on the books, 18 Beechcraft Model 17s were delivered in the calendar year 1934; 37 Beechcrafts were delivered in 1935, with 60 employees then on the payroll.

C17 series

Introduced in February 1936, the first C17B (NC15812) saw the drag flaps again placed forward of the ailerons on the underside of the lower wings and the angle of incidence of the horizontal stabilizer was changed, easing longitudinal trim (Fig. 3-9). An additional rear fuselage fuel tank to the five-tank option of the B17B and L models increased total fuel to 166 gallons, and the resulting still-air range to over 1,000 miles.

The C17L was similar except for the engine installation. The Models C17E and C17R retained the upper wing drag flaps and were fitted with two fuselage

Douglas D. Olson

3-8 The last of 15 Model B17Rs (NC15817) was delivered to Fred C. Talbot, Hilsboro, California on April 5, 1936, in a smart blue and yellow color scheme. Impressed as 42-52999, it survived the war, but as NC47833 was lost in a hangar fire in 1946.

3-9 Serving as a demonstrator with the O.J. Whitney Air Service, New York, this Model C17B (NC16439) was completed August 19, 1936. Impressed in World War II as 42-97426 until disposed of in October 1944, it was last registered to Josephine E. Becker, New York, as NC46291.

3-10 Ordered by racing pilot Frank Hawks, this supercharged 600-hp Pratt & Whitney R-985 Wasp Jr.-powered Model D17W (X17081) was not put into production. Note the large cowl scoop. It was impressed as a U.S. Navy GB-1 (BuNo.09776) in World War II.

and one lower wing fuel tank for 98 gallons, with the option of three more 23–25 gallon wing tanks for a total of 173 gallons.

One hundred and seventy-five employees delivered 61 Beechcraft Model 17s in 1936, and the Company was incorporated in September of that year. In January 1937, business was so good that Walter Beech was able to purchase the production site and factory buildings at East Central, Wichita, from Curtiss-Wright. An administrative office block and additional hangar space were then erected. A total of 67 Beechcraft model 17s was delivered in 1937, including the first for the United States Navy.

D17 series

The first of the uprated D17W models (NX17081) was built in 1937 to the order of Frank Hawks (Fig. 3-10). It was powered by a special 600-hp Pratt & Whitney R-985-SC-G Wasp Junior. When Pratt & Whitney decided not to market this engine, a 450-hp Wright R-975 was fitted and the aircraft was redesignated D17R and built in modest numbers.

The Model D showed some significant changes to the earlier Beechcrafts. The fuselage was some 18 inches longer and a new windshield profile was adopted. The ailerons were relocated to the upper wings with plain flaps located on the lower wings. Both these surfaces were later balanced. The wing section was changed to the NACA 23012 airfoil and plywood wing panels outboard of the I-struts were added later to stiffen the structure against possible flutter.

The tail was now a cantilever unit and the elevators were later to have external metal balance horns; a trim tab on the rudder became standard (Fig. 3-11). New shock absorbers were fitted to the undercarriage legs and toe brakes were standard. Two fuselage and one low wing tank totalled 102 gallons, with the option of fitting the three remaining wing tanks for a total of 174 gallons.

A second special 600-hp Pratt & Whitney R-985-SC-G-powered D17W (R18562) was completed in 1937 for Miss Jacqueline Cochrane, and she used it to set several speed and altitude records. The 350-hp Wright R-760-E2 Whirlwind-powered D17A (NC19453) saw limited production (Fig. 3-12), but large numbers of the 450-hp Pratt & Whitney Wasp Junior-powered Model D17S were produced for both civil and military orders.

At least two D17Ss (N51969 and N2277Z) had their fuselage structures reworked by their postwar owners to all-metal; these proved to be some 90 pounds lighter and had slightly better performance (Fig. 3-13). Another D17S (N79484) sports a three-bladed propeller on its Pratt & Whitney Wasp Junior engine (Fig. 3-14).

Peter M. Bowers

3-11 The Beechcraft Model D series featured a lengthened fuselage, which improved handling on the ground and in the air. Ailerons were fitted to the upper wings and plain flaps replaced the decelerator flaps of the earlier models. Note the cantilever horizontal stabilizer. External balance weights were later added to the elevators. This Model D17S (N18028) is the second production aircraft and is currently owned by Bernard A. Yocke, Prestbury, Illinois.

Museum of Flight

3-12 The Wright R-760 powered Model D17A (NC19453) saw limited production. This Beechcraft was impressed as a UC-43F in May 1942, survived the war and is now owned by John L. Harbor, Central Point, Oregon, registered N50959.

3-13 At least two Model D17S had their fuselages recovered in metal by their postwar owners. These proved to be some 90 pounds lighter and showed a slightly improved performance. N51969 at Merced, June 8, 1969.

3-14 Sporting a three-bladed propeller on its Pratt & Whitney R-985 Wasp engine, this Model D17S (N79484) is owned by Gene E. Moser, Monterey Park, California. Shown at Merced, June 7, 1980.

Variations and Production **27**

E17 series

To meet continuing orders for the cheaper, lower-powered Beechcrafts, the 1937 E17B model was produced (NC17085). Although it followed the D17's arrangement of wing control surfaces, retained the braced tail unit of the C17 model (Fig. 3-15). Standard fuel was 77 gallons in one fuselage and two lower wing tanks, with the option of two upper wing tanks for a total of 125 gallons. Toe brakes replaced the dreaded Johnson bar lever, much to the relief of owner-pilots who, when taxiing, were not keen on juggling the tasks of holding the control column back, placing the other hand on the throttle, and then having to pull the bar from time to time for braking. The only Model E17L (R343) was completed for the military in Argentina.

F17 series

The last of the prewar single-engined Beechcrafts was the Model F17D (NC18786) introduced in 1938. It was of similar configuration to the E17 series with a braced tailplane, but had the more powerful 330-hp Jacobs (R-915) L-6 engine (Fig. 3-16).

Peter M. Bowers

3-15 Production of the cheaper, lower-powered Beechcrafts continued in 1937 with the Model E17B/L. It had the aileron and flap arrangement of the Model D but retained the braced horizontal stabilizer of the earlier models. NC17085 is a Model E17B at Oakland, California, March, 1941. It was impressed in WWII as 42-56087, disposed of as NC57830.

3-16 The 1938 Model F17D (NC20797) was structurally similar to the Model E but had the higher-powered 330-hp Jacobs L-6 engine. This one was impressed during WWII as 42-107411, now owned by Richard Miller, Brighton, Colorado.

Total prewar production

In 1938, sales exceeded $1 million and 53 Model 17s were delivered. Seventy-five more single-engined Beechcrafts were delivered in 1939, including 10 to the U.S. Navy and U.S. Army Air Corps. The years 1940 saw production of the civil Model 17s decreasing, with only 31 delivered. Six more were delivered in 1941 and the last four prewar civil Beechcraft Model 17s were delivered in January 1942, making a total of 353 civil and military single-engined Beechcrafts built since 1932.

Aileron/elevator controls

The arrangement of aileron/elevator control wheels was varied. Although twin control wheels on a T or Y bar were common, a single throw-over wheel could also be specified (Figs. 3-17 through 3-19).

Colors and markings

Beechcraft customers were invited to specify the color finish for their new Model 17s, and purchasers chose a range of fuselage colors with one, three, or even five fuselage stripes in a contrasting color. Dopes and paints were supplied by Berry Brothers of Detroit, Michigan; Merrimac Chemical of Boston, Massachusetts; and the Glidden Company, Cleveland, Ohio.

The distinctive birdstripe marking first appeared on the new twin-engined Beechcraft Model 18 in 1936 and was soon seen on production Model 17s.

3-17 The arrangement of the Model 17's elevator/aileron control wheels varied. Here are twin wheels on T-bar, shown in a Model D17S (N114H).

3-18 A Y-bar in a Model F17D (N46296).

3-19 Single "throw-over" type control wheel shown in a Model D17S (NC17679).

A Loening Yellow fuselage with the birdstripe in blue or black was chosen by many purchasers.

Records of all the prewar paint schemes have been preserved, including the customer drawings prepared by Beech employee Pat Curry. One of the more demanding schemes was that applied to the Model D17S (NC18776) ordered by racing pilot Ross Hadley (see Chapter 4). The scheme was in the same colors as the Stearman C3B biplane he had flown since the early 1930s. He specified Commanderie Green above the centerline of the fuselage with Consolidated Blue below. The wings were also painted in Consolidated Blue, and the blue engine cowl was finished in his "star" pattern with a red "meatball" in the five-pointed military star. The Glidden's Light Vermillion Red fuselage arrow was outlined in white, separating the Green and Blue colours. A U.S. flag was painted on the rudder. Following World War II, Mr. Hadley had his replacement Model D17S (NC53298) painted in a similar color scheme (Fig. 3-20).

Substitute engines

Research has shown that in later years many Beechcraft Model 17s received replacement engines of a different type than originally fitted. An example of

Douglas D. Olson

3-20 Racing pilot Ross Hadley ordered his postwar Model D17S (NC53298) finished in the same colours as his prewar Model—Commanderie Green above and Consolidated Blue below the fuselage centerline, wings also finished in Consolidated Blue. The blue engine cowl was painted with his "star" pattern. The fuselage arrow was in Glidden's Light Vermillion Red outlined in white, separating the green and blue. This aircraft is now owned by Dick Perry, Hampshire, Illinois.

this is the C17B (NS17064), which left the factory in 1937 with a 285-hp Jacobs L-5. When operated later as an aerial photographic platform, it was fitted with a 330-hp Jacobs L-6MB, becoming a C17D. In 1966, with a private owner, it became a C17L when a 225-hp Jacobs L-4 was installed. The present owner expects to complete the restoration of this Beechcraft with a 420-hp Wright R-975, changing the designation again—this time to a C17R!

With prewar piston engines hard to find in wartime New Zealand, at least one Model B17L (NZ573/ZK-AEU) had its factory-fitted engine replaced by a 220-hp Continental W670/6A. Postwar in the U.S., a 300-hp Lycoming R-680-E3B radial was installed in an F17D in 1949 (NC20789), and in 1952 a similar engine was installed in a C17B (NC17061).

Seaplanes and an amphibian

The Beechcraft Model 17 series was certified to operate on floats and skis. The first floatplane to be delivered was a Model SB17L (NC15402) for Thomson Airways operating from Baltimore, Maryland (Fig. 3-21). The Beechcraft fuselage was corrosion-proofed and the floats fitted were Edo Model 38-3430s with water rudders. These weighed in at 452 pounds and a special gross weight of 3,525 pounds was authorized for the Model SB17L. At least 16 Beechcrafts were operated on floats (Fig. 3-22).

3-21 The first Beechcraft seaplane was this Model SB17L (NC15402) delivered to Thomson Airways, Baltimore, Maryland, in November, 1935. The floats were Edo Model 38-3430. Note the large ventral fin. At least 16 Beechcraft floatplanes were flown.

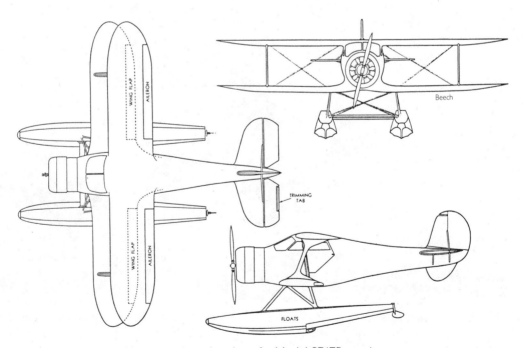

3-22 Three-view drawing of a Model SE17B seaplane.

The sole amphibian, a Model C17B (NC16440) fitted with Edo Model 49-3875 floats, sported twin main and tailwheels and a large ventral fin. Wheeled landings proved unacceptable, and the conversion was abandoned (Fig. 3-23).

Wartime production

World War II production of the Model D17S was under both U.S. Navy and U.S. Army Air Force contracts, totalling 412 Navy GB-2 and USAAF UC-43 aircraft. Capital for construction and operating wartime production was obtained from the Reconstruction Finance Company and wartime Beechcraft Model 17s were built in a 50,000 square foot factory at the south end of the Beech airport.

Lend-Lease deliveries of GB-2/UC-43 aircraft to the Brazilian Air Force totalled 31, while the British Royal Navy and Royal Air Force received a total of 105 Model 17s from USN and USAAF Contracts.

The Beech Aircraft Corporation and its employees were awarded the Army/Navy "E" for Excellence Award five times during World War II.

Model G17S

With a return to peace in 1945, Beech took the last of the pre-war Model D17S Beechcrafts (NC21934) and engineered several improvements for the postwar market (Fig. 3-24). The engine mounting for the 450-hp Pratt & Whitney R-985

3-23 The sole Beechcraft amphibian, a Model C17B (NC16440), shows twin main and tailwheels fitted to the Edo floats. Note the large ventral fin. Wheeled landings proved unacceptable and the conversion was abandoned.

Wasp Junior was extended, and a new, drag-reducing cowl and exhaust system fitted. Standard fuel was two fuselage plus two lower wing tanks for 124 gallons, with the option of two upper wing tanks for a total of 170 gallons. A revised windscreen improved the fuselage line and the vertical fin and rudder were redesigned with additional area for more positive control. New landing gear fairings were attached and a new instrument panel was fitted, along with improved interior furnishings.

35 Bonanza

The introduction of the new all-metal Beech Model 35 Bonanza (Fig. 3-25), with a price tag of only $8,000, overtook the high construction costs of the labor-intensive Model G17S. In 1948, the Henry Seale Aviation Supply Company in Dallas, Texas, offered for sale the last five of the post-war model G17S airplanes from parts assembled by Beech. The last Staggerwing delivery was in 1949.

3-24 The last Model D17S (NC21934) was repurchased by Beech in 1945 and re-engineered for the postwar markets as the Model G17S. Note the drag-reducing engine cowl, new line of the windshield, larger vertical fin and rudder, and new undercarriage doors. List price of the Staggerwing was $29,000 and only 20 were built.

3-25 The new postwar all-metal Beech Model 35 Bonanza was offered for only $8,000, bringing to an end the production of the Beech Staggerwing. This is the prototype Bonanza (NX80040), first flown December 22, 1945.

Table 3-1. Beechcraft Model 17

Year	Model	Power		Weight	Cruise mph	feet	Cost	Number built
1932/3	17R	420 hp	Wright R-975-E2	4500	170		$19,000	2
1934	A17F	690 hp	Wright R-1820-F11	5200	225		24,500	1
1935	A17FS+	710 hp	Wright SR-1820-F3	6000	215 @ 5000		30,000	1
1934/6	B17L	225 hp	Jacobs R-775(L-4)	3150	162 @ 5000		8,000	46
1934	B17B	285 hp	Jacobs R-830(L-5)	3150	177 @ 7200		9,000	1
1935	B17E	285 hp	Wright R-760-E1	3263	177 @ 7200		12,980	4
1935–6	B17R	420 hp	Wright R-975-E2	3600	202 @ 9000		14,500	15
1936–7	C17B	285 hp	Jacobs R-830(L-5)	3150	177 @ 7200		9,250	39
1936–7	C17L	225 hp	Jacobs R-775(L-4)	3150	166 @ 7200		8,550	6
1936–7	C17R	420 hp	Wright R-975-E2	3900	202 @ 1000		14,500	17
1936–7	C17E	285 hp	Wright R-760-E1	3600	177 @ 7200		13,450	2
1937–40	D17R	450 hp	Wright R-975-E3	4200	202 @ 9700		18,870	26
1937–42	D17S	450 hp	P + W R-985-SB	4200	202 @ 9700		18,870	68
1939	D17A	350 hp	Wright R-760-E2	4200	180 @ 9600		16,350	8
1937	D17W	600 hp	P + W R-985-SC-G	4200	225 @ 13500		20,600	2*
1937–40	E17B	285 hp	Jacobs R-830(L-5)	3350	177 @ 7200		10,490	54
1937	E17L	225 hp	Jacobs R-775(L-4)	3350	166 @ 7200		9,690	1
1938–42	F17D	330 hp	Jacobs R-915(L-6)	3550	182 @ 10000		13,980	60**
1946–49	G17S	450 hp	P + W R-985-AN4	4250	201 @ 10000		29,000	20

+ Supercharged engine.
* One converted to a D17R
** Total prewar Model 17 production was 353 including military variants.

Table 3-2. Genealogy

1932/33	1934	1935	1936	1937	1938	1939	1940/42	1942/45	1945/9
17R	A17F	A17FS							
	B17L	B17L	C17L	E17L					
	B17B		C17B	E17B	E17B	E17B			
			B17E	C17E	C17E				
			B17R	C17R	D17R	D17R	D17R		
					D17S	D17S	D17S	D17S	UC43/GB2	G17S
					D17W				
							D17A		
						F17D	F17D	F17D	

4

Racing and sporting Staggerwings

Walter Beech had always had an eye for air races and for winning them, too, so it was not surprising to find Beechcraft Model 17s appearing on air race programs for 1933 and later years.

Miami 1933

Only some eight weeks following its first flight at Wichita, the prototype fixed-gear Model 17 (NC449N) was flown to the All-American Air Maneuvers at Miami in January 1933 to enter the race for the coveted Texaco Trophy. The Beechcraft was the only new aircraft at Miami that had not been seen at the Cleveland Races the previous year.

At the start of the race, pilot Eric H. Wood used all his skills to take the prototype Beechcraft safely into the air, using throttle and rudder to balance the torque of the powerful 420-hp Wright Whirlwind engine against the narrow track of the panted landing gear. He found that the negative stagger of the wings really did give an advantage in visibility when turning the pylons and overtaking other aircraft. Wood's skills and the performance of the Beechcraft were rewarded with first place in the Texaco Trophy Race, crossing the finish line at an average speed of 163 mph for five laps of the five-mile closed course.

Howard Hughes

The first Model A17F Beechcraft (NC12583), powered by a 690-hp Wright R-1820-F11 engine, was delivered to Goodall Worsted Company in May 1934,

Sandford Mills, Minnesota, which manufactured VELMO fabrics, mohair frieze, and suede velvet as used in U.S. rail cars and automobiles for more than 50 years. These products were now used for the interior furnishings of the new Beechcraft. Painted in black, red, and cream, this Beechcraft was flown by Robert S. Fogg. Walter Beech had hoped he would enter this model in the 1934 MacRobertson England-Australia Air Race, but in November the Beechcraft was sold to Howard Hughes, who wanted a "hot ship" to familiarize himself with the high performance and demanding landing characteristics of the Wright Cyclone-powered biplane before the initial test-flying of his H-1 Racer. The experience was put to good use during the test flying and successful world speed record attempt of the Hughes Racer.

In 1937, the A17F, now owned by Mr. Harold Smith, President of the American Liquid Gas Corporation, was entered in the Bendix Air Race as race number 64. Marked *Ring-Free Red Streak* (Fig. 4-1), it was flown by Robert "Bob"

4-1 The first Beechcraft Model A17F (NC12583) was flown by the Goodall Worsted Company, Sandford Mills, Minnesota (and later by Howard Hughes). Entered as Race 64 and marked *Ring-Free Red Streak* in the 1937 Bendix Trophy Race by Bob Perlick, flown in the 1938 Bendix by Perlick as Race 85, but didn't finish. It was destroyed by fire in 1944.

Perlick. When flagged for takeoff, Perlick turned onto the Burbank runway and opened the throttle in his nonstop attempt to reach Cleveland. The overloaded "flying gas tank" slowly picked up speed into the light westerly wind, but as fuel sloshed back and forth in the cabin tanks, the Beechcraft lurched about the pavement. With a scream of protest from the tires, the gear collapsed and the Beechcraft sank to the runway. Perlick scrambled out, but there was no fire.

After a rebuild by the Timm Aircraft Company, Glendale, California, Perlick made another attempt in the same A17F as race 85 in 1938; as the cabin was full of extra fuel tanks, he had to climb in through a cockpit window to take his seat at the controls! Although he took off safely, Perlick ran out of fuel and was forced down at Woodriver, Illinois.

MacRobertson Race

The last of the panted, fixed-gear A-17FS Beechcrafts was powered by a 710-hp supercharged SR-1820-F3 engine and, registered NR12569, was entered in the 1934 MacRobertson England-Australia Air Race as race number 57. Walter Beech had selected Louis Thaden and Frank Hawks as his race pilots, and they hoped to cruise at 15,000 feet and 220 mph enroute.

Despite the extra fuel tanks it was realized that for a long-distance race, range was more important than speed, and after calculating the time to be lost at the number of fuel stops planned, the entry was withdrawn. Painted a striking Cherry Red, silver, and blue, the Beechcraft was sold to the Bureau of Air Commerce in July 1935 and as NS-68 (Fig. 4-2) was flown by them until dismantled some two years later.

Museum of Flight

4-2   The last panted, fixed-gear Model A17FS (NR12569) was entered for the 1934 MacRobertson England-to-Australia Air Race. Withdrawn and sold to the Bureau of Air Commerce as NS-68, it was dismantled in 1937.

Charlotte Frye

Pioneer racing aviatrix Mrs. Charlotte Frye of Griffin, Georgia, bought the first production Model B17L (NC270Y) with retractable gear in February 1935 and flew it extensively until 1942 (Fig. 4-3). She won the All-American Air Maneuvres at Miami, December 12–14 1935, and was the first woman to be sworn in by the U.S. Post Office to fly the air mail in Georgia in her Beechcraft. On May 19, 1938, she flew about 1100 pieces of mail from Griffen to Atlanta, Georgia, in her Beechcraft to commemorate the 20th Anniversary of the air mail. She autographed one of the pictures of her Beechcraft with the words: "I sincerely wish all pilots knew the ease of maneuvering a Beechcraft. Beauty and speed speak for themselves." Both she and her sturdy biplane survived at least two forced landings. The first required two new wings, landing gear, and a tail structure. In the 1936 Miami Air Races, she suffered an engine failure after takeoff and put her Beechcraft down in a swamp three miles out from the airport.

More sporting sales

Beechcraft Model 17s were chosen as sporting aircraft by several racing personalities. Frank Hawks flew a blue-striped red Model B17L (NC14409), and

4-3   The first Model B17L (NC270Y) was flown for eight years by Mrs. Charlotte Frye. Entered in the 1935 and 1936 Miami Air Races, it carried the air mails in Georgia in 1938. Restored "as new" in 1982, it is now on display at the Beech Delivery Centre, Wichita, Kansas. Smithsonian/Beech

Miss Arlene Davis owned a similar cream-and-red Model 17 (NC15400), race number 33, in which she won the 50-mile Woman's Handicap in the 1934 National Air Races. In a letter to Walter Beech, she commented: "I find it the easiest plane I have ever piloted, including my previous plane. Thanks to you for the simply marvelous performance you have been able to obtain."

Max Constant won the 1935 Macfadden Race from Floyd Bennett Field, New York, to Miami, Florida, at 204.77 mph. Louise Thaden set a National Women's Speed Record over 100 kilometers on May 29, 1936, in a C17R at the St. Louis International Air Races, with a speed of 197.958 mph. Roscoe Turner flew an Insignia Blue Model F17D (NC19492) with the "birdstripe" in Loening Yellow.

Winning the Bendix

Pride of place among the many racing successes of the Beechcraft Model 17 must be Louise Thaden and Blanche Noyes's unexpected win in the 1936 Bendix Race. Both girls were based on the West Coast, implementing the Bureau of Air Commerce's Air Marketing Program. This involved the survey and painting of VFR air route beacons on prominent landmarks and buildings across the United States to assist the safe routing of general aviation, air mail, and passenger flights. Back in Wichita, Olive Ann Beech was keen to see a female success in air racing and after Vincent Bendix had offered a special $2,500 prize for the first women to finish the race, she phoned Louise and asked her to fly a stock Model C17R in the race.

Taking Blanche Noyes with her as copilot, Louise travelled to Wichita to find a sleek new Beechcraft finished in Sherwin Williams Blue with white markings. A large race number 62 had been painted on the side of the fuselage and the regular NC number had been replaced by R15835, indicating a "Restricted" license due to the extra 56-gallon fuselage tank and additional oil supply Walter Beech had installed to see them through the long legs of the 2,450-mile race (Fig. 4-4). The Beechcraft carried only a radio receiver and primary flight instruments for the transcontinental flight.

Arriving at Floyd Bennett Field, New York, with their Beechcraft for the start of the race, Louise and Blanche watched the other contestants preparing their entries—Laura Ingalls in her sleek Lockheed Orion, William "Buster" Warner and W.S. Gulick in the big Vultee V1A, Benny and Maxine Howard's *Mister Mulligan*, George Pomeroy in the twin-engined Swiflite-marked Douglas DC-2 transport, Amelia Earhart and Helen Richey in their Lockheed Vega, and Joe Jacobson, who was frantically looking for a parachute to stow in his Northrop Gamma.

With the race departures scheduled for the early morning, both women went out to the apron to find their Beechcraft already being warmed up by

4-4 Louise Thaden and Blanche Noyes had an unexpected win flying this Beechcraft Model C17R (R15835) to first place in the 1936 Bendix Trophy Race. Later delivered to the Government of Honduras (11), it is rumored to still exist. Smithsonian/Beech

Louise's husband, Herbert von Thaden. He had also plotted the transcontinental route to Los Angeles on their charts. With the latest wind and weather forecasts aboard, Louise Thaden and Blanche Noyes took the heavily laden Beechcraft into the air, climbing slowly above the overcast to find clear weather on top.

Ninety minutes later, anxious to check their ground speed and drift, Blanche Noyes tried to tune the receiver to a ground beacon, but found too much static. Then suddenly, through a gap in the clouds, she saw one of her air markers on a barn roof! Spiraling down, they found themselves over Circleville, Ohio, only a few miles off track and making a good ground speed of 210 mph on a lean 65 percent power. Climbing back to their best cruising altitude of 8,000 feet, they continued on course for St. Louis, but here the weather report was bad. Kansas City was also reporting below limits, so they continued to their alternate stop at Wichita. Walter Beech was waiting with fuel and refreshments—and news that the Howards' *Mister Mulligan* and the Douglas DC-2 were already refuelled and ahead.

In less than ten minutes the Beechcraft had taken on 169 gallons of fuel and 12 gallons of oil and was back in the air (narrowly avoiding a landing Army plane) and setting course for Los Angeles. Louise and Blanche, knowing they had no chance of winning, were still eager to finish the race, and, climbing to 14,000 feet, crossed the high peaks of the Continental Divide, where they found headwinds of 60 mph reducing their ground speed to 135 mph. Letting down to 12,000 feet on the western side of the mountains lessened the headwinds, but they became anxious that they would not reach Los Angeles before the 6:00 P.M. deadline on September 4th.

Starting an early cruise descent toward the coast, they found themselves entering a layer of smoke from adjacent forest fires and, with the late afternoon sun in their eyes, searched desperately for Mines Field. Suddenly they saw the Bendix pylon, turned and raced across the finish line from the west, head-on to the Marine Corps display pilots in their Vought Corsairs. As they touched down at 5:09 and taxied away from the grandstand, men were waving and cars were streaming across the field towards them.

"I wonder what we've done wrong *now?*" Louise said to Blanche.

Then they heard the cry: "You've just won the Bendix Race!"

Their winning time of 14:55:01 at an average speed of 165.346 mph put them 45 minutes ahead of Laura Ingalls, who had been delayed refueling at Wichita. *Mister Mulligan* had crashed north of Crownpoint, New Mexico, and Joe Jacobson had been thrown clear and descended by parachute after his Northrop Gamma exploded in flight near Stafford, Kansas. Both women gasped when they were handed their prize money—$4,500 for first place plus the special award of $2,500 for the first women over the line.

To highlight their success and further publicize the Model 17, Walter Beech offered Louise a job at the factory and as a demonstration pilot sent her on a celebration tour around the United States in a "lookalike" Beechcraft—the winning C17R had been sold before the race to the government of Honduras (11) to replace an earlier Model B17L! The next available C17R (factory number 81) was completed in the same colour and markings and flown as the "Bendix Winner." It survives today.

Other races

Further racing successes of the Beechcraft Model 17 have been summarized in the late Reed Kinert's *Racing Planes* and Robert T. Smith's *Staggerwing* books. In the 1936 Miami All-American Races, a C17B won the Colonel E.H.R. Green Trophy Race at 185 mph, beating another Beechcraft flown by Bob Glass of Dallas, Texas, to second place.

At the Mile-High Air Races at Denver, Colorado, in July that year, Bill Ong flew the Beechcraft that would later win the Bendix Race to first place in the Frank E. Phillips Trophy Race, covering the ten laps of the five-mile closed course at an average speed of 191.971 mph. Of the five aircraft to be placed, three were Beechcraft Model 17s, which prompted the comment, "It takes a Beechcraft to beat a Beechcraft." A D17R, flown by Art Chester, won the same race in 1937 at St. Louis, Missouri.

In the 1937 Bendix, Jacqueline Cochrane flew her green and orange D17W (R18562) marked 13 to third place (Fig. 4-5), averaging 194.74 mph. Max Constant came fourth in the same aircraft, marked 31, in the 1938 and 1939 races (NX18562), averaging 199.330 and 231.366 mph, respectively. Ross Hadley,

Peter M. Bowers

4-5 This supercharged Pratt & Whitney-powered Model D17W (R18562) was flown to third place in the 1937 Bendix Trophy Race by Jacqueline Cochrane. Note the cowl scoop. It came fourth in the 1938 and 1939 Bendix Races, flown by Max Constant. Again flown by Jacqueline Cochrane, it set Women's Speed and Altitude records. Impressed as a UC-43K (42-107277) during World War II, it is believed to have crashed in Sweetwater, Texas, as NC50958.

William T. Larkins

4-6 Ross Hadley flew this dazzling Model D17S (NC18776) to fifth place in the 1938 Bendix Trophy Race. Impressed as a UC-43B (42-38324) in March 1942, it survived the war but crashed June 20, 1976, Amarillo, Texas. Shown here at Alameda, 1939.

with Al Larry as copilot, came fifth in the 1938 Bendix, flying his new dazzlingly painted D17S, race number 44 (NC18776), to average 181.842 mph (Fig. 4-6). William Maycock made sixth place in the 1939 race flying an all-silver D17S with blue trim, race 66 (NC20768).

Nominated as the "most outstanding woman flier in America," Louise Thaden was awarded the Harmon Trophy in 1936. The following year, she continued her record-setting days in the Beechcraft, with an inter-city distance record of 40 minutes 23 seconds for the 125 miles from Detroit to Akron, Ohio, on January 21, 1937.

The association of Jacqueline Cochrane and her Model D17W continued when she set a new Women's World Speed Record of 203.895 mph over a 1,000-kilometer course on July 26, 1937. Two days later, she set another record of 200.712 mph over a 100-kilometer course. A later success in the Beechcraft was her new altitude record of 30,052 feet on March 24, 1939, at Palm Springs, California.

To emphasize the "fail-safe" practicalities of a retractable undercarriage (Fig. 4-7), Walter Beech had a Model C17B (NC15838) specially prepared for the 1936 National Air Races in Los Angeles. Two skids were fitted to the under-

4-7 This gear-up landing of a Model B17L (NC14455) in 1936 demonstates the "fail-safe" characteristic of the Beechcraft. This Staggerwing was last reported with the Carter Motor Co., Greensboro, North Carolina, in 1955.

side of the Beechcraft, and with a special brake to stop the propeller horizontally, Bill Ong flew daily demonstrations to show the safety of the Beechcraft when landed with its gear retracted. These demonstrations were again staged at the 1937 Miami Air Show.

Using the Beechcraft for a different purpose, a Model E17B (NC16449) was flown in Europe from May 1937 until December 1938 by New York beautician Gloria Bristol.

Racing revival

In postwar years the Beechcraft biplane faded from the competition scene until the Reno Air Races of 1970. There, following the cancellation of the North American AT-6 races due to a disagreement between Reno management and AT-6 spokesmen, a Beech Staggerwing Exhibition Race was flown on each of the last three days of the event. The late air race historian Reed Kinert noted: "With all due credit to the beautiful aircraft themselves, these exhibitions were about as interesting as watching paint dry." Well, it must have been a fine finish for those pilots flying their treasured Beechcraft Model 17s!

William T. Larkins provided a listing and photographs of the participants in the September 18, 1970, *Exhibition Race* (Fig. 4-8, and 4-9):

4-8 Leaving the line of warbirds at Reno in 1970, Bert Jensen in his Model D17S (N46810) sports race number 11 and clocked an average 153mph in the Staggerwing Exhibition Race.

Marking	Model	Race	Pilot	mph
N80317	G17S	77	Bryant L. Morris, Portuguese Bay, CA	153.191
N46810	D17S	11	Bert Jensen, Crystal Bay, NV	153.011
N1184V	D17S	44	Donald E. Clark, Mammoth Lakes, CA	148.794
N9885H	D17S	9	Phillip Livingston, Seattle, WA	142.105
N70E	G17S	7	Noel Gourselle, Sacramento, CA	140.870

TransAtlantic Race

The following year a Canadian Model D17S Staggerwing (CF-GWL) was one of the competitors in the 1971 Trans-Atlantic Air Race from Abingdon, England, to Vancouver, British Columbia, Canada. The 5,787-mile race offered prizes of $120,000 and was sponsored by the Royal Trust to commemorate the Centenary of the Canadian Province of British Columbia. The Staggerwing, race 12, sported a Royal Blue fuselage with day-glow orange wings and stabilizer. It was flown eastbound to England for the start of the race, via Greenland and Iceland, by Air Canada pilot Myron Olson and owner George Le May.

4-9 Philip Kent Livingstone's Model D17S (N9885H), marked Race 9 at the 1970 Reno Air Races, went on to fly in South America, and in 1976 across the North Atlantic to Europe in a round-the-world attempt. It is currently based in Anchorage, Alaska.

Competitors were allowed to choose any trans-Atlantic route, and were credited with a 60-minute allowance for each of up to five certified landings between Abingdon and Quebec City. One of the five landings had to be at Goose Bay, Gander, Sydney or Halifax.

Again following the Northern Route across the Atlantic, Olson and Le May reached Quebec City 3,306 miles and 25 hours after leaving Prestwick, Scotland, and were ready for a well-earned rest. Their final placing at Vancouver—seventh out of 13 in Class C—was all the more commendable in that they had the oldest airplane in the event and had competed against modern piston and turbo-prop entries (Fig. 4-10).

Phillip K. Livingston was one of several postwar pilots to fly the North Atlantic in his Staggerwing (N9885H) in July 1976, attempting an eastbound round-the-world flight via Europe, Africa, India, and the Far East to Alaska. The flight was abandoned on the island of Corfu after the gear collapsed.

In December 1976, Robert C. Ellis, from Barranquilla, also abandoned an

4-10 This Model D17 (CF-GWL) was flown by Myron Olson and owner George Le May from Abingdon, England, across the North Atlantic to Vancouver, winning seventh place in Class C during the 1971 British Columbia Centenary Celebrations. It is shown departing Prestwick, Scotland, on the evening of July 1.

eastbound round-the-world flight in his Staggerwing (N69217) at Abu Dhabi in the Middle East after engine and fuel tankage problems showed the trans-Pacific legs of Wake to Hawaii to California were too far for the already-overloaded Staggerwing.

Mr. Livingstone, of Anchorage, Alaska, was one of 136 entries in the Bicentennial Around Australia Air Race, which took place in September–October 1988. Assigned race number 90, his plans were scrapped when he could not complete the enroute diplomatic clearances in time.

Dr. Rolph A. Versen of Rockford, Illinois, flew his newly acquired Staggerwing (N9405H) across the Atlantic to Germany in May 1987, using the Northern Route. Mr. Heinz G. Peier followed in August 1988, flying his Model D17S (N582) to his home in Switzerland.

7-

5

Commercial
and
exploration use

The oil exploration, drilling, and marketing industry was to play an important part in the early fortunes of the Beech Aircraft Company with the purchase of several models of the Beechcraft biplane as a fast and comfortable means of transportation.

Oil birds

The first fixed-gear Model 17R Beechcraft (NC499N) was delivered to the Ethyl Corporation in May 1934, after modifications to a wider track landing gear, swiveling tailwheel, and a closed-type engine cowl. Drag flaps were fitted to the underside of the upper wings in place of the split rudder, and a new black-and-orange paint scheme was applied (Fig. 5-1). Flown by Dewey L. Noyes, the prototype Beechcraft Model 17 was nearly destroyed in a fatal crash near Nunda, New York, on December 11, 1935, after encountering icing conditions.

Prior to this, the second Model 17R (NC58Y) had been purchased in July 1933 by Tom Loffland of the Loffland Drilling Company of Tulsa, Oklahoma. This sale is said to have carried the Beech Company through their first year of operation. This aircraft was flown by company pilot Eddie Ross until the early summer of 1935, when it was traded for a later model. The Loffland Brothers later bought four more Beechcrafts.

The last of the fixed-gear Model A17FS Beechcrafts was flown by the Bureau of Air Commerce (NS68) as a high-speed transport until it was dismantled in 1937.

Museum of Flight

5-1 The first fixed-gear Model 17R (NC499N) as delivered to the Ethyl Corporation in May, 1934, modified with a wider track gear, swivelling tailwheel, baffled cowl, and new paint. Decelerator flaps have been added to the underside of the upper wing.

John P. Gaty, a commercial pilot, bought the second Model B17L, finished in bright Loening Yellow overall with black trim. Gaty's acquaintance with Walter Beech led to his appointment on March 1, 1937, as Vice-President of the company and Director of Sales. This Beechcraft (NC12584) was sold to Socony-Vacuum Oil. With their marks—"Aero Mobiloil" and the "Gargoyle" symbol in red on the cream fuselage—the plane was shipped to Europe in August 1934 as deck cargo for a tour by W. Faust, Director of Aviation Sales, and H.J. White (Fig. 5-2). Demonstration flights were made in England from Reading and Heston aerodromes. The company bought a second Model B17L later, which was flown by R.W. Brown.

Standard Oil of New Jersey operated two "STANAVO" Beechcrafts (NC12592 and NC289Y)—finished in a striking Fokker Red fuselage with silver wing color scheme—as high-speed corporate transports. A similarly painted C17B (NC15840) was delivered to Mr. E.E. Aldrin of the Standard Oil Development Company of New York (Fig. 5-3). (Mr. Aldrin's son, Edwin "Buzz" Aldrin, would later accompany Neil Armstrong on the Apollo 11 mission to the moon in July 1969.) This Model C17B is now displayed in the National Air and Space Museum.

Harry A. Hammill of Republic Oil, Houston, Texas, not only used the Beechcraft for company business but became a Beech distributor with many sales successes. Other early Beechcrafts were flown by Lion Oil Refining, El Dorado, Arkansas (NC15403); Continental Oil, Ponca City, California (NC15413); and King Oil, Wichita Falls, Kansas (NC15813). The first Model C17R (NC15487) was

Peter M. Bowers

5-2 In 1934, the second Model B17L (NC12584) was shipped to Europe for a demonstration tour flown by Aero Mobiloil Director of Sales W. Faust and H.J. White. Note the "long" main gear. This aircraft was later lost in a crash at Minneapolis before World War II.

Smithsonian

5-3 Painted in a striking Fokker Red and silver wing color scheme, this C17B (NC15840) was flown for Standard Oil by Mr. E.E. Aldrin, father of astronaut Edwin "Buzz" Aldrin. It is now displayed in the NASM, Washington, DC.

flown by Oil County Specialities (OCS) of Coffeyville, Kansas (Fig. 5-4).

An early Model B17E (NC14458) was bought by James Marshall Murray, President of the ME-TEX Oil Supply Company of Hobbs, New Mexico, replacing an earlier Waco biplane. Company pilot Charles C. Spencer was charged with building an airport from which to operate and located a section of land one mile square (640 acres) west of the town. A disused warehouse was relocated to the site as a hangar, and a corrugated iron building served as home. Three runways were laid out and the rest of the land was turned over to the town as an airport. The new Beechcraft served the company well with flights into Texas and Mexico before being replaced by a more powerful Model B17R (NC15814). When Charles Spencer retired some 40 years later, he bought a surplus U.S. Navy GB-2 (NC44561), which was housed alongside his home in Los Altos, California.

The C17B model bought by Wilcox Oil and Gas of Tulsa, Oklahoma, (NC17072) was later purchased and flown by *Staggerwing* author Robert T. Smith. It is still flown by Staggerwing Club member Tom Switzer from his home in Baltimore, Ohio. Another C17B (NC17079) was flown by Illinois Oil of Dallas, Texas, while Lloyd Noble Drilling in Tulsa, Oklahoma, operated five single-engined Beechcrafts from 1937 through 1946.

Olson Drilling purchased the first Model D17S (NC17081) from Harry A Hammill. Other D17S models were flown by Emperor Oil of Fort Worth, Texas

Peter M. Bowers

5-4   The first Model C17R (NC15487) was flown by the Oil Country Specialities Manufacturing Company, Coffeville, Kansas. Burned in a hangar fire in 1968, Chad N. Koppie of Gilberts, Illinois, has the remaining wing panels.

(NC18582). Tom Graham Oil, Corpus Christi, Texas, flew two Beechcrafts (NC18584 and NC18577). The Texas Company flew two "Texaco Red" Beechcrafts (NC19494 and NC21905) for several years.

H.J. Mosser Oil flew a Loening Yellow F17D model (NC20789) from their Alice, Texas, base and Shell Aviation flew their Stinson Green Model D17A (NC21906) from 1940 through 1946.

The last of the prewar Beechcraft Model 17s (NC21934) was painted overall in Army and Navy Orange with the birdstripe in Berry's Consolidated Blue, outlined in white. It was flown by Ohio Oil and later repurchased by the Beech Aircraft Corporation for conversion into the first postwar Model G17S.

Swiflite Aircraft of New York had the NC number 2000 assigned to their red Model C17R, which was flown by company pilot George Pomeroy.

World War I fighter pilot and noted author Col. Elliot White Springs of Springs Cotton Mills, Lancaster, South Carolina, was a regular flier of a Diana Cream and blue Model F17D (NC285Y), and later an all-silver Model D17S (NC21902). Colonel Springs is particularly remembered for the editing and publication of *War Birds*, the diary of an "unknown" aviator (in fact, John MacGavock Grider).

U.S. government Staggerwings

The United States Department of Commerce and the Civil Aeronautics Administration operated a fleet of Beechcrafts from 1935 until the early postwar years (Fig. 5-5). The states of Maine, New Jersey, Connecticut, and Indiana all used the Beechcraft biplanes for forestry control and surveys of their states. The registration numbers of these aircraft were prefixed NS, indicating non-military use by the federal government or a state agency.

During 1939, the CAA used four Beechcraft Model 17s to investigate possible wing failures caused by aileron flutter. Several accident investigations since 1936 had asked the question "Was flutter a contributory cause?" when placarded speeds or loads had been exceeded or very turbulent air encountered. The facilities of the Civil Aeronautics Administration, the National Advisory Committee for Aeronautics, and the Materiel Division of the Army Air Corps were combined to look at the problem. These tests—on a Model C17R (NC2), a Model D17S (a U.S. Navy GB-1), a Model E17B (NC91), and a Model F17D— were made independently and at different times. The results were then compared, discrepancies discussed, and final conclusions reached.

The effective remedial measures for preventing flutter in the Beechcraft Model 17 biplanes were published in NACA and Air Corps reports and were executed by Beech Service Bulletins No. 74, 75, and 76. The B17 and C17 models were to have their ailerons statically balanced by adding lead weights ahead of the hinge line. The D17, E17, and F17 models had increased torsional

Museum of Flight

5-5 The Civil Aeronautics Administration operated a fleet of Beechcrafts from 1935. This Gliddens Black and Galatea Orange Model B17L (NS66) was flown by the CAA, and later Stinson Aircraft. Shown at Portland, Oregon, July 21, 1935. Postwar, the wings and fuselage of this Beechcraft were used to rebuild another B17L (NC14408).

stiffness applied to the wingtip sections by the addition of plywood panels outboard of each I strut and the ailerons and flaps were statically balanced as noted above.

Commercial passenger operations

The prewar equivalent of Third Level Operations—flying passengers into "hub" airports for their connecting flights to distant destinations—was often undertaken with speedy Beechcraft Model 17 aircraft.

Ozark Airlines, the first to be incorporated in the State of Missouri, replaced their high-wing Fairchild and Stinson monoplanes in 1944 with four Model F17D Beechcrafts to operate a two-flights-per-day triangular route—Springfield to St. Louis to Kansas City to Springfield—scheduled service in both directions.

These feeder services proved popular with passengers, but as the airline was not federally certificated, passengers could not be transported over the state boundary. The pilots not only flew the aircraft, but acted as ticket and baggage men and in-flight attendants. The single-engined Beechcrafts often beat the scheduled times of the TWA DC-3 transports between St. Louis and Kansas City. By the autumn of 1945, however, twin-engined Cessna UC-78s became available and replaced the Beechcrafts. Although slower than the single-engined biplanes, passenger loads were greater and they had the reassurance of a multi-engined transport.

In South America, the speedy Beechcraft biplanes were operated by Na-vegaceo Aerea Brasiliera from 1941 on the coastal air route to Recife. Postwar, Linea Expresa Bolivar C.A. flew their Beechcraft YV-C-LBQ on routes in Bolivia.

Charter and air taxi operators were all keen users of the fast, comfortable Beechcraft biplane. Aviation stunt flier Paul Mantz used a Model C17L for several years to fly movie stars to Las Vegas and Reno for both gambling and divorces. This Beechcraft (NC16441) also starred in several motion pictures, including the 1938 MGM release *Too Hot to Handle* with Walter Pidgeon and Myrna Loy (Fig. 5-6). It was later to serve the Civil Air Patrol flying from Biggs Field, El Paso, Texas, on a three-times-per-day patrol from El Paso to Douglas, Arizona, and El Paso to Moffitt, Texas, searching low-level for infiltrators or suspicious activ-

Smithsonian/Beech

5-6 Studio set picture of Walter Pidgeon and Myrna Loy with Beechcraft Model C17L (NC16441) during the filming of the 1938 MGM release *Too Hot to Handle*. It was then owned by Paul Mantz and later flown by the Civil Air Patrol, now registered N962W and on display at the Staggerwing Museum Foundation, Tullahoma, Tennessee.

ities. Re-registered N962W, this Model C17L is currently on loan to the Staggerwing Museum Foundation.

The Beechcraft Model 17 has not always been on the right side of the law. In March 1983, FBI agents seized a Model D17S (N1178V) at the South Columbus Airport, Ohio, after they arrested the pilot with one pound of cocaine in his possession. This Staggerwing was later donated by the federal authorities for permanent display at the U.S. Navy Museum in Pensacola, Florida (Fig. 5-7). Commenting on the drug-smuggling activity in a classic biplane, Staggerwing Museum Foundation Treasurer Robert Graves was quoted by *The Columbus Dispatch*: "As a plane for a drug runner, he could not have picked anything much more conspicuous."

Other uses

The stable, high-altitude performance of the single-engined Beechcraft was recognized by several pre- and postwar aerial survey and exploration companies, with Edgar Tobin, Kargl, and Abrams Aerial Surveys, together with the National

5-7 This Model D17S (N1178V) was seized by federal agents after they arrested the pilot in possession of drugs. It was donated to and now on display at the U.S. Navy Museum in Pensacola, Florida.

Geophysical and Seismograph Companies all operating prewar models. Gordon "Rocky" Warren of Western State Aviation, Gunnison, Colorado, operated two Model D17S Beechcrafts (N28A and NC9290H) in postwar years, the Pratt & Whitney Wasp Junior engines of which were fitted with 14:1 blowers (Fig. 5-8). These allowed U.S. Geological Survey flights up to altitudes of 31,000 feet and caused several incredulous jet pilots to report to Air Traffic Control: "We have just passed a red biplane cruising at Flight Level Two Five Zero!"

The aircraft and motor service industries were fond users of the Beechcraft too, and Model 17s were used by Wright Aeronautical, Pratt & Whitney, Chevrolet Motor, Champion Spark Plugs, Prest-o-Lite, Bowers Battery, Firestone, and the General Tire & Rubber companies.

Antarctic adventure

For a project much farther afield, the Chicago-based Research Foundation of the Armour Institute of Technology purchased a Beechcraft Model D17A (NC20778) to accompany the Antarctic Service Expedition in 1940. Five years earlier, while serving with the second Byrd Antarctic Expedition, Scientific Director Dr. Thomas C. Poulter proposed a "Snow-Cruiser" that would provide

William T. Larkins

5-8 Flown by Gordon "Rocky" Warren, Gunnison, Colorado, this Model D17S (N28A) was fitted with a supercharged Pratt & Whitney R-985 Wasp Jr. engine and used for U.S. Geological Survey flights. It frequently operated up to 31,000 feet.

a mobile home for members of the U.S. Antarctic Service and a transport vehicle for the survey Beechcraft. When completed, the 75,000-pound transporter and the Beechcraft (Fig. 5-9) were loaded aboard the USS *North Star* at Philadelphia and set sail for the Great Ice Barrier in Antarctica.

The transporter proved to be a failure, however; its large tires sank into the soft snow and the gearing of the diesel engines was found to be unsuitable. A land site was therefore established at West Base, Little America, from which the Beechcraft could operate effectively. This it did with remarkable reliability in temperatures down to −71F (−57C) from its first flight on January 26, 1940. It made more than 60 sorties before the expedition returned in February 1941 (Fig. 5-10).

Expedition pilot Technical Sergeant Theodore A. "Pete" Petras (USMC) had first flown the Beechcraft to the Naval Aircraft Factory at Philadelphia for the fitting of skis and cold weather equipment. It was then flown to Boston to be loaded aboard ship for the Antarctic. The flight log of the Beechcraft is displayed at the Staggerwing Museum Foundation and shows three phases of the operation. Initial flight tests from the Antarctic base included testing and calibrating the ADF homing device (Fig. 5-11). This was followed by photographic and mapping sorties over Little America, the Rockfeller and Alexandra Mountains, the Bay of Whales, the Queen Maud Range, Mt. Flood and beyond, and the unknown coast to East McKinley. Several high-altitude flights up to 21,000 feet were made recording cosmic ray activity. Ground parties established caches

Beech

5-9 The projected 75,000-pound transporter with Beechcraft and pilot used by the Research Foundation of the Armour Institute of Technology in the 1940 Antarctic Service Expedition. It was not a success in the soft snow conditions.

5-10 This Model D17A (NC20778) flew more than 60 sorties for the Antarctic Service Expedition during 1940–41. Here it is taxiing for takeoff on skis from the base in Little America, Antarctica with the USS *Bear* in the background, April 1941.

of fuel for the Beechcraft, which supported the longer flights as shown on December 9, 1940, when Sgt. Petras and Dr. Siple took off from West Base and landed at Rockefeller Mountain to top off with fuel. They then flew east to Sultzberger Bay and the fog-filled valley between Mt. Haines and Mt. Rea. After refueling at Mt. Rea, they continued east to photo-survey the Mt. Hal Flood area, which ranges from, 5,400 to 9,000 feet high. They then dropped supplies to a ground party before landing at Mt. Grace McKinley for fuel—then on to a fourth landing and a brief conversation with Dr. Wade before returning to West Base after a 13-hour mission.

A less successful mission was with Dr. Paul Siple, when they attempted to fly to the South Pole, pilot Petras taking along a three-foot candy-striped bar to leave as a memento! Unfortunately, a blizzard hid their halfway cache of fuel and they had to return short of their goal.

Finally, the Beechcraft was dispatched to aid the Marine Corps Curtiss R4C-1 Condor twin-engined transport (Bu9584), which had forced-landed at 7830S 15730W following engine failure. A radio call brought the Beechcraft out to the site with a spare cylinder. While repairs were attempted, pilot Petras and radio operator Gray completed the supply mission of the Condor. On their return they learned that repairs were hopeless, so the three Condor crewmembers were flown in the Beechcraft back to base.

On January 3, 1941, two flights in the Beechcraft were made to return the

5-11   USMC Pilot Theodore "Pete" Petras and the Beechcraft (NC20778) being warmed up before flight in Little America, Antarctica. Note the Curtiss R4C Condor twin-engined transport.

crew to the downed Condor. Six days later, two more flights were made to pick up the crew and equipment after the decision was made to abandon the Condor. Searches were also made, unsuccessfully, for a lost dog team.

The Beechcraft was also prepared for loading aboard the USS *Bear* for a possible rescue attempt of the personnel from East Base who were still frozen in by solid ice packs that prevented ships from entering the area. The second Condor of the Expedition was used to fly these men in two parties to a 300-foot precipice above the sea on Watkins Island, where they were lowered to the USS *Bear* below. The Condor transport was abandoned on the island. With the completion of the last Antarctic flights, the Beechcraft was loaded aboard the USS *North Star* on January 31, 1941, for its return to the United States, and was then sold to Australia.

Ted Petras continued his service with the U.S. Marine Corps to the rank of Colonel. In 1944, he was the first pilot to land an Allied aircraft (a twin-engined Beech JRB) on New Britain Island since the evacuation of Royal Australian Air Force Wirraway aircraft after the Japanese invasion in January 1942.

6

Foreign civil use

Many of the adventurous and far-ranging exploits of the single-engined Beechcraft biplane were performed by the examples sold outside of the United States.

In 1936, Mr. O.J. Whitney, the Beech distributor and air charter operator based at Jackson Heights, New York, accompanied by Burham Litchfield of Fairchild Cameras, took an early Model B17L (NC15409) on an extended three-month tour of South America (Fig. 6-1). They totalled 165 flying hours and made 600 takeoffs and landings, including demonstrations. So successful were they that the Beechcraft was sold in Argentina to begin a local interest in Beech aircraft that continues to this day.

Whitney and Litchfield left New York in the 225-hp Jacobs-powered Beechcraft and flew down the East Coast, making good use of the Fairchild-Kreusi radio-compass installation. They left Miami on January 5, 1936, crossing the Caribbean to the 5,000-foot airport at Guatemala City. After stopping off in the Central American states, they touched down on the 8,700-foot airfield at Bogota before continuing to Quito in Ecuador, landing at an altitude of 10,000 feet. They flew the length of Peru to Santiago before climbing to 17,000 feet to cross the Andes Mountains into Argentina.

After demonstrations in Rio De Janeiro, Brazil, the Beechcraft returned to Buenos Aires. There it was sold to Dr. Samuel Bosch, who later handled all the Beech sales in Argentina. To highlight the economy of operation of the Model B17L, Whitney averaged a 177-mph cruise using only 14 gallons of gasoline an hour—over 12 air miles per gallon!

Capt. Otto Thaning, the Danish Consul in Johannesburg, South Africa, was also a 1934 purchaser of the Model B17L, replacing his de Havilland Puss Moth.

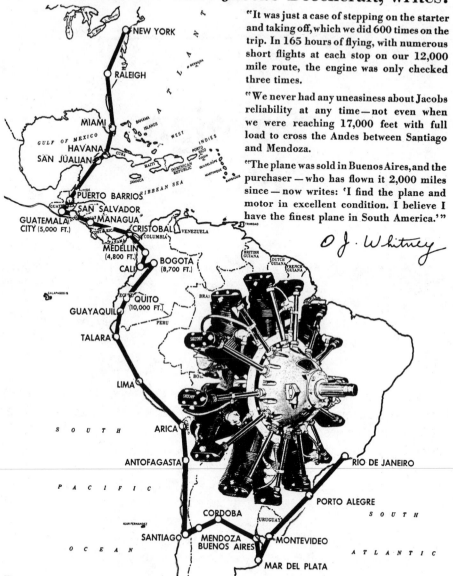

Mr. O. J. Whitney, who flew the trip shown on the map in a standard 225 H.P. Jacobs Beechcraft, writes:

"It was just a case of stepping on the starter and taking off, which we did 600 times on the trip. In 165 hours of flying, with numerous short flights at each stop on our 12,000 mile route, the engine was only checked three times.

"We never had any uneasiness about Jacobs reliability at any time—not even when we were reaching 17,000 feet with full load to cross the Andes between Santiago and Mendoza.

"The plane was sold in Buenos Aires, and the purchaser—who has flown it 2,000 miles since—now writes: 'I find the plane and motor in excellent condition. I believe I have the finest plane in South America.'"

O. J. Whitney

JACOBS AIRCRAFT ENGINE CO.
POTTSTOWN, PENNSYLVANIA

JUNE 1936

7

6-1 Route of O.J. Whitney's flight in a Model B17L (NC15409) from New York to Rio de Janeiro in 1936. Total flying time was 165 hours, including 600 demonstration takeoffs and landings. The aircraft was sold to Dr. Samuel Bosch in Buenos Aires. Aero Digest

Both were registered ZS-BBC. After an accident in September 1936, the original engine and propeller of this Beechcraft were used in a replacement Model C17L, also registered ZS-BBC. During the Winter War of 1939-40, Captain Thaning presented this same Beechcraft to the Finnish Air Force (BC-1) and it survived military operations to continue in civil use as OH-PKA.

Mexico to England—the long way round!

The longest recorded flight of a Beechcraft 17 was undertaken in 1935, with the 50th aircraft built. A Model B17R (G-ADLE) was flown from Mexico to London, England, via Canada, Russia, China, India, and the Middle East, a distance of some 21,000 miles. The owner-pilot, Captain Sir Harold L. Farquhar, serving as First Secretary at the British legation in Mexico City, had traded in an earlier Model B17L (XB-AIZ) for this more powerful Beechcraft. He was accompanied by Fritz Beiler, a WWI German pilot living in Mexico (Fig. 6-2). The handwritten diary of this flight seems to indicate a conflict of goals between the two. Capt. Farquhar was content with a "pleasure cruise" around the world, while Fritz Beiler was eager to make the fastest time and set a record. The delay caused by bad weather over the Bering Straits resolved the issue, however, and the flight continued as a "leisurely jaunt" to London (Fig. 6-3).

The Beechcraft left Mexico City on August 16, 1935, and was flown to College Point, Long Island, to have seaplane floats attached by the Edo Aircraft Company. Its landing gear was not removed, but was retracted into the fuselage, to be used later, after the floats were discarded. With additional survival equipment and spares aboard, a gross weight of 3,972 pounds was reached before the 162 gallons (990 pounds) of fuel were added. For later takeoffs in smooth water conditions, some fuel had to be offloaded.

Ten days later, after servicing by O.J. Whitney at North Beach Airport, New York (now La Guardia), the flight took off from the harbour ramp and set course across Canada. Beech engineer Ted Wells had calculated that at 9,000 feet and at a setting of 24.5 inches of manifold pressure, their cruising speed would true out at 150-mph. Careful leaning of the mixture reduced fuel consumption three to four gallons per hour and resulted in safe enroute times in excess of eight hours. Because only 73-octane fuel was available after leaving Canada, the forward fuselage tank was filled with 80-octane and used for all takeoffs.

Following the delay in crossing the Bering Strait, the flight continued with overnight stops across the southeast coast of Siberia and by an amazing coincidence, they overflew the remains of the Lockheed Vega (NR869E) flown by Jimmy Mattern on his solo round-the-world attempt of June 1933. The Beechcraft rode out an overnight 50-mph gale while moored along the coast and the pilots experienced some takeoffs in heavy rain, 1/4-mile visibilities, and cloud

6-2 The round-the-world Model B17R (G-ADLE) of Sir Harold L. Farquhar and Fritz Beiler was fitted with Edo floats at New York before departure. The landing gear had been retracted and was used later in the flight after the floats had been removed.

ceilings on the surface. Their navigation and the range and altitude of the Beechcraft caused little problem, however, and it was at Harbin that a Japanese Air Force crew assisted the conversion to a landplane. Capt. Farquhar alighted the Beechcraft alongside a mud flat in the river and 60 coolies built a sand wall under the lower wings, removed the floats, and prepared a makeshift runway for the takeoff. With only a light load aboard, the Beechcraft took off easily and Farquhar landed at the nearby aerodrome to tidy up the conversion.

As a landplane, the Beechcraft could now be routed overland to Peking, Shanghai, and Hong Kong, where Capt. Farquhar experienced some rather unfriendly British colonialism! For the first time, landing fees and hangarage had to be paid here, "but nothing was charged for the well-meaning efforts of the Army wireless expert to service the Lear radio—it hasn't functioned since!"

With accurate weather reports from the French in Indochina, the flight continued, stopping off to visit the Lost Kingdom of the Khmers at Ankor. Leaving Bangkok, they crossed India via Calcutta, Allahabad, and Jodhpur, where they found a "model" airport with runways and floodlights. Continuing via Bombay and Karachi, they landed at Gwadar, where Stanavo stocked 80-octane fuel. Then came a long (8:30) flight to Basra and on to Baghdad. On this leg the air temperature resulted in cylinder head temperatures of 420 degrees F and Farquhar had trouble keeping the oil temperature within limits.

At Luxor, Bieler was taken ill and while in the hospital, Capt. Farquhar used his best diplomacy to get a personal letter of recommendation to cross Italian Libya from General Balbo. Following a personal inspection from the General, they left Tripoli and after a refueling stop at Tunis, crossed the Mediterranean to Marignane, France.

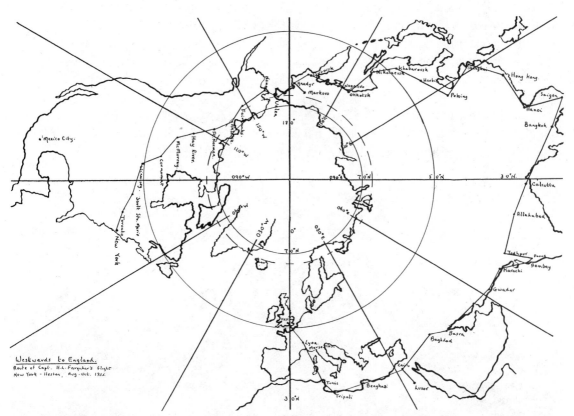

6-3 Route of the Model B17R (G-ADLE) from New York to Heston, England, in 1935. The 21,000-mile trip was completed in two months of demanding flying. The floats were removed at Harbin by the Japanese and the Beech continued as a landplane to England.

Flight magazine briefly recorded their arrival in England: "Mr. H. Farquhar, landed at Heston, London, in his Beechcraft at 11:46 on Oct. 29, 1935, after a trans-Asiatic-European holiday flight."

European Model 17s

The following year, a single-engined Beechcraft 17 was to fly the North Atlantic nonstop from New York to Frankfurt without starting the engine! Loaded into the cargo hold of the German airship LZ-129 *Hindenberg,* this Model B17R (NC15816) was transported to Europe on the ship's second crossing in May 1936, with James and Mae Haizlip and their son James (Fig. 6-4). They planned to beat a series of inter-city speed records set earlier by Frank Hawks flying the Travel Air Model R "Mystery Ship" *Texaco 13.* The Beechcraft was demonstrated at Lympne aerodrome on the South Coast of England in August 1936.

Following the tour, the Beechcraft was sold to the Italian airline Ala Littoria in April 1937 (I-IBIS) and was based at Urbe airport, Rome. It is reported to have been used to transport the exiled King Alfonso of Spain to Austria at the start of the Spanish Civil War. Stored during World War II, it was restored in 1947 by Mr. Klinger, the retired president of the airline, who used it for long flights through Europe and the Mediterranean until sold to a publicity company in 1948.

Four Beechcrafts were sold to England: a Model B17L (G-ADDH) to the long-distance aviatrix Mrs. Amy Mollison, a B17R (G-ADLE) to Sir H.L. Farquhar and used on his previously described round-the-world flight, and two Model

Beech

6-4 The first aircraft to be transported across the North Atlantic by air, this Model B17R (NC15816) was carried aboard the German airship *Hindenberg* on its second transAtlantic flight in 1936. It was demonstrated in Europe by Jimmy Haizlip before being sold to Ala Littoira and registered I-IBIS.

C17Rs flown by sporting pilots Charles E. Gardner (G-AENY) and Jimmy Haizlip (G-AESJ). Gardner's Beechcraft (Fig. 6-5) was based at his private aerodrome at Warlingham, Surrey, alongside the Percival Vega and Mew Gulls in which he won the King's Cup Air Races in 1936 and 1937. As American-built aircraft were barred from the annual King's Cup Race, Gardner demonstrated the high performance of the Beechcraft by flying three passengers from London to Paris in one hour and two minutes.

Jimmy Haizlip had some difficulty with British Customs when uncrating G-AESJ, which was due to be exhibited at the 1937 Brussels International Aircraft Exhibition. Having overcome the difficulty of re-exportation, the Dutch agent F. ten Bos completed the London-to-Brussels flight in 58 minutes (Fig. 6-6).

War casualties

The conflicts in Ethiopia and Spain saw the demise of several foreign Beechcrafts. A Model B17L (NC14405), sold to the Emperor of Ethiopia for photographic and dispatch services, was delivered by air from France in 1935, but was destroyed at Akaki during an Italian air attack the following year.

During the first few days of the Spanish Civil War (which began on July 18,

Beech

6-5 Flown by the English racing pilot Charles Gardner, this Model C17R (G-AENY) was based at his private aerodrome in Warlingham, Surrey. Later registered F-APFB, it may have ended its days serving in the Spanish Civil War.

1936), there was a Beechcraft at Burgos, piloted by an Englishman. It disappeared without a trace after being sent on a war mission.

It is believed that the first three British-registered Beechcrafts found their way to the Republican forces in the Spanish Civil War, where they joined a B17L (EC-BEB) that had been used by an air taxi company. A B17R was sold to Rene Drouillet in Paris, France, and allotted F-APFD. He was the aero adviser to Emperor Haile Selasse of Ethiopia. This last Beechcraft was alleged to have been involved in a plot, financed by the Italians, to kidnap the Emperor. The French authorities refused permission for the flight to the war zone, but it became unnecessary when the government of Ethiopia collapsed.

This Beechcraft eventually appeared, still with its U.S. markings (NC15811), with the Spanish-funded Air Pyrennes in 1937. It was reported to have been used for reconnaissance flights in the Spanish Civil War and to have evacuated the pro-Republican President Aquirre. Named *The Negus,* its back was painted with the coats of arms and emblems of the countries where it had served, several states in the U.S., the Lion of Judah, and the Basque Nation. French

Museum of Flight

6-6 First shown at the Brussels Air Show in 1937, this Model C17R (G-AESJ) was later flown by the air survey pioneer Sydney Cotton. Impressed into the RAF as DS180 during WWII, it was scrapped after an accident in January 1944.

pilot George Lebeau flew it. When the Germans took control of southwestern France in November 1942, they discovered the Beechcraft in a dismantled condition. It was taken to Paris and displayed in the captured aircraft collection without its propeller or wings. The collection is thought to have been destroyed in an Allied air aid in 1944.

On the other side of the world, in Dutch Borneo, a dedicated gentleman, the Reverend George Fisk, successfully flew a Beechcraft Model SE17B seaplane (PK-SAM) in support of the Christian and Missionary Alliance work in bringing Christianity to the native Dyak peoples. Operating from swift-flowing rivers cut into the steeply wooded terrain, the all-yellow Beechcraft biplane proved a reliable and speedy form of transport from its arrival in late 1939 until burned by the Dutch in 1942 to prevent its capture by the advancing Japanese.

Beechcrafts down under

The first of seven Beechcrafts to be registered in Australia, a Model B17L (VH-UXP), was delivered in November 1936 to Thomas Masse in Sydney. This was followed by a Model C17B (VH-UYI) for John F. Jackson in Queensland, which was later lost in an accident in May 1941. A Model F17D (VH-ACU) was delivered to Charles Wilfred Russell, also in Queensland.

Following its return from the U.S. Antarctic Expedition in 1941, the Model D17A (NC20778) was offered by Beech Aircraft to E.J. Connellan of Alice Springs, to be registered as VH-AFP. By the time the Beechcraft arrived in Australia, both it and the remaining two earlier arrivals were impressed into the Royal Australian Air Force as A39-1 to A39-3. All three survived the war.

The New Zealand Model B17L (ZK-AEU) arrived in Auckland on December 23, 1936, aboard the SS *City of Manchester* (Fig. 6-7). It was found to have been damaged in transit, but was repaired and delivered to the Auckland Aero Club in May 1937. A major part of the purchase price had been funded by the St. John's Ambulance Association and the Beechcraft served as a speedy air ambulance with typical flight times of 1:50 from Auckland to the capital, Wellington. It survived the war and is now being restored in Australia as VH-TOT.

Asiatic Beechcrafts

In 1936, a license to manufacture the Beechcraft Model 17 in Japan was granted to the Japan Air Transport Company of Tokyo. The first Model C17E (NC15836)

Smithsonian/Beech

6-7 Flown by the Auckland Aero Club on behalf of the St. Johns Ambulance Service, this Model B17L (ZK-AEU) was impressed as NZ573 in WWII. It survived the war and is currently being restored in Australia as VH-TOT.

was delivered in August and parts for a second Model C17E were delivered in December as a "copy" model. Beechcrafter Virgil Adamson went with the aircraft to Japan to supervise assembly. A total of 20 licence-built Beechcrafts were completed and flown by the Japan Airways Company (Fig. 6-8).

Indian National Airways bought five Model E17Bs in 1938/39 (VT-AKJ, -AKK, AKL, -ALN and -ALV), which were based in New Delhi and were operated along the route Karachi—Lahore—New Delhi in support of the Empire Air Mail Scheme (Fig. 6-9). Tata Air Lines in Bombay bought a Model D17S (VT-ALY) in 1940 to assist their air mail service along the route to Karachi and Columbo. A postwar Model G17S (VT-CIT) was delivered to Tata in 1946 and was later used by Associated Airworks, Calcutta, for charter flights to the tea plantations.

Canadian bush flying

Some of the most demanding bush flights were those made by the single-engined Beechcrafts operated in Canada during the prewar years. Usually flown from water with floats or with skis fitted for the winter snows, Mackenzie Air Services operated a C17R (CF-BBB) on floats from Edmonton, Alberta, along the Mackenzie River to Lake Athabasca (Fig. 6-10). Specializing in servicing the mining industry, this Beechcraft was known as *Brintnell's Bastard Beech,* linking the three letters of the registration with the name of managing director, Leight Brintnell.

Starratt Airways flew a similar staggering (CF-BIF) from Hudson, Ontario. Midland Airways operated a D17S (CF-BLU) from Calgary, Alberta, and Noorduyn Aircraft in Quebec flew a E17B (CF-BHA) from the St. Lawrence River, Quebec. The Canadian Department of Transport in Ottowa flew three Model D17S

Peter M. Bowers

6-8 One of 20 Wright R-760-powered Model C17E Beechcrafts built under licence by the Japan Air Transport Company of Tokyo. Beechcrafter Virgil Adamson help set up licence production in Japan.

Smithsonian/Beech

6-9 Indian National Airways bought five of these Model E17Bs to serve the Empire Air Mail Scheme out of New Delhi. They were finished silver overall with Consolidated Blue trim. VT-AKJ was lost in a collision in 1939.

6-10 This Model C17R seaplane (CF-BBB) was painted in light green and gold with a silver Birdstripe. It served its Canadian owners well until lost in a takeoff accident in 1955.

(CF-CCA, DTE, and DTF). All survived the war except CF-BLU, which has been leased to Canadian Airways and was lost in the Northwest Territories in 1942, when it hit a sandbar and overturned.

Central and South America

In addition to Sir H.L. Farquhar's Model B17L (XB-AIZ), two Wright-powered Beechcrafts (XA-BEV and XA-BKO) were operated by Aeronaves de Mexico in 1938-39 from Mexico City to Acapulco. A Model F17D (XB-AGO) was flown by Henry B. Hanson for a Mexican Mining company and Senor Leopoldo Lopez flew a Model D17S (XB-AKT) for Marias de Chihuahua.

An early delivery in 1935 was a Model B17L (CZ-116) to Isthmian Airways, Ancon, Canal Zone. This was replaced by a similarly registered Beechcraft in 1939.

Following Whitney's demonstration of the Beechcraft, four civil models were imported and flown in Brazil, including a C17B by Count Raul Crispi from Sao Paulo (PP-TCQ), a D17S (PP-NAC) flown by Navegacao Aerea Brasileira (NAB) on the coastal route to Recife, and another D17S (PP-TGE) flown by Senor Assis de Chateaubriand from Rio de Janeiro. The F17D (PP-FAA) flown

6-11 This Model D17S (PP-FAA) was flown by the Department of Aeronautics, Rio de Janiero, Brazil, and later served with the Brazilian Armed Forces as FAB.2819. It was struck Off Charge in December, 1955.

by the Department of Civil Aviation was later to serve with the Brazilian military forces (Fig. 6-11).

A Beechcraft Model 17 was operated by Transportes Aereos Ranqueles in Argentina on routes from Cordoba during 1940, flying three services a week.

A Model B17R (NPC-28) was delivered to Manila in December 1935 and flown by the Philippine Aerial Taxi Company. Two Beechcrafts, a Model C17B (C-49) and a Model F17D (C-48), one of which was named *General Prez*, were flown out of Bogota, Colombia, by Captain Hans Hoffman for Aerovias Ramales Colombianas (ARCO), along routes in the Llanos region of eastern Colombia, until taken over by SCADTA in 1941. An unidentified Beechcraft Model 17 (CC-CAA) was flown in Chile.

U.S. and foreign military service

Military Beechcraft Model 17 biplanes were acquired from two sources—direct purchases from the factory and impressements from civilian owners during 1941 and 42.

Much confusion has been caused to the aviation buff because of the random mix of military UC-43/GB-2 production, many aircraft having dual U.S. Navy and U.S. Army Air Force serial numbers, with additional serial numbers assigned to deliveries to China, Brazil, and Great Britain under Lend-Lease.

The United States Navy first purchased a Model C17R in December 1936, designated JB-1 (Utility Beech), which was delivered to the Naval Air Station Anacostia, DC, and given the Bureau of Aeronautics serial number 0801 (Fig. 7-1). A further 10 Beechcraft Model D17S, designated GB-1 (transport, single-engined, Beech), were delivered in 1939–40 to serve with the major Naval Air Sations (NAS) throughout the United States and abroad as the first production military Beechcraft Model 17s (Fig. 7-2) as follows:

BuNo. 1589 NAS Anacostia, DC.
1590 NAS Norfolk, Virginia.
1591 Naval Air Attache, Mexico City.
1592 NAS San Diego, California.
1593 Naval Attache, Madrid, Spain.
1594 NAS Pensacola, Florida.
1594 NAS New York, New York.
1898 Naval Aircraft Factory VX-3D4.
1899 NAS Corpus Christi, Texas.
1900 General Inspector of Naval Aircraft, New York.

Douglas D. Olson

7-1 The U.S. Navy's first Beechcraft was this Model C17R delivered in December 1936 and designated JB-1 (BuNo.0801). Assigned to NAS Anacostia VX4DS in 1937, it carries a Captains's epaulette rank card.

Douglas D. Olson

7-2 This U.S. Navy GB-1 (BuNo.1591) was delivered June 16, 1939 and flown by the Naval Attache in Mexico City. It was stricken at Corpus Cristi April 15, 1943.

The United States Army Air Corps took delivery of three Beechcraft Model D17S biplanes in 1939, designated VC-43 (Fig. 7-3). These "Service Test—Cargo" biplanes were assigned to US Air Attaches as follows:

AC.39-139   London, England.
AC.39-140   Paris, France.
AC.39-141   Rome, Italy.

A large number of single-engined Beechcrafts were impressed into U.S. Navy and U.S. Army Air Force service as GB-1, GB-2, and UC-43 transports, the Navy taking 11 and the Army Air Force acquiring 118 from their civilian owners. Many of these survived the rigors of wartime flying and returned to civil use.

The impressed UC-43s served with numerous USAAF service and manufacturing units and many ended their days being taken apart and reassembled as instructional airframes at the military training schools. Three more served with the War Training Service in Washington, DC, Santa Monica, California, and Chicago, Illinois. At least one UC-43B (42-38233) served with the 14th Air Force in Karachi, and two UC-43Cs (42-97048 and 42-107414) served with the North Atlantic Wing, Air Transport Command, during the summer of 1943. Three served with the 16th Photo Squadron, based at Bolling and Norfolk Fields (Fig. 7-4). A number were released from the USAAF to the Civil Aeronautics Administration to continue their busy lives before returning to private owners in 1945.

Peter M. Bowers

7-3 One of three U.S. Army Air Corps YC-43s, 39-139 was assigned to the Air Attache, London, England. Impressed into the RAF as DR628, it survived the war and is now owned by Bruce R. McCaw, Belleview, Washington, as N295BS.

7-4 Rare takeoff shot of an impressed UC-43G (43-68855) at Boeing Field. This was the first Model C17B (NC15812) and was used by Edgar Tobin Aerial Surveys. It served at Hensley, Casper, and Bolling Fields before being relegated to an instructional airframe at the Medford Vocational School.

7-5 Sporting the Naval Air Transport Service badge on the cowl, this Model GB-2 (12334) had been assigned to the Base at Terminal Island. It's shown here at Concord, California, November 20, 1946. As N9885H, it was later to race at Reno and is owned by Philip Kent Livingstone, Anchorage, Alaska.

Restored to authentic wartime Royal Air Force colors, N18V masquerades as Prince Bernhart's PB-1 and DR628. The yellow triangle on the front fuselage was an indicator of lethal gas contamination.

Parked at Prestwick International Airport, Scotland, this Model D17S (CF-GWL) was positioning for the Trans-Atlantic Air Race in July 1970.

PHOTO BY ROGER W. BUNCE

The first production model of the Beechcraft Model 17, this B17L (NC270Y) was first flown February 2, 1934. It was delivered to Mrs. Charlotte Frye and flown by her until 1942. After several post-war owners, it was purchased and restored by Richard Perry and Richard Hanson. It is now on display at the Beech Delivery Center, Wichita, Kansas.

Delivered to Capitol Airlines on July 22, 1936, this B17L (NC14417) later suffered three gear-up landings and a cabin fire. It was purchased by Tom Rench, Racine, Wisconsin, in 1969. Restoration was completed ten years later.

The arrangement of the elevator/aileron control wheels varied from the twin-wheels on the "T" bar of a Model D17S (N114H) and "Y" bar in a Model F17D (shown, N46296), to the single "throw-over" type, also on the Model D17S (NC17679).

The updated instrument panel of the Model G17S N44G. A stable platform in IFR weather conditions, the Staggerwing is a delight to fly.

Resplendent in its original US Army Air Corp colors as a YC-43, the 295th Beechcraft (N295BS) is now based at Bellevue, Washington. It had a long career with the USAAC, the Royal Air Force, and civilian owners in England, Southern Rhodesia, South Africa, and the United States.

On display in the Staggerwing Museum Foundation, Tullahoma, Tennessee, is this Model C17L (NC962W), factory serial 100. Flown by Paul Mantz in pre-war years as NC16441, it starred in several movies. It has been restored and repainted in the original green with orange trim by its present owner, Alton Cianchettie.

The clean cowl of Bill Halverson's Model G17S (NC80316) leads a lineup of Staggerwings at the 1988 Annual Convention in Tullahoma, Tennessee. Note its more ''solid'' undercarriage doors.

Compare the fins and rudders of the Model G17S (N44G) with the earlier D17S (NC67550). Both also show the cantilever horizontal stabilizer and elevator mass balance weights.

PHOTO BY ROGER W. BUNCE

This Model E17B was first delivered August 15, 1937, to Daniel R. Topping in New York registered as NC17092. It was impressed during World War II as 42-53006 and survived to become N50650. It has been rebuilt and is now owned by Robert Kreutzer, San Diego, California. It is shown outside the Beechcraft factory (June 1977).

PHOTO BY ROGER W. BUNCE

This Model F17D was delivered to Joseph James Ryan in New York City, January 18, 1939, as NC18574. It passed through several post-war owners as N124D and N500SW and is now registered N139KP to Peachey & Peachey Farms, Hugoton, Kansas.

U.S Navy and Army purchases of production GB-2 and UC-43s were not delivered until 1943 (Fig. 7-5), and many of these were assigned under Lend-Lease to the British Royal Air Force and Royal Navy, to China, and to the Armed Forces of Brazil.

Staggerwings to China and Brazil

The Military Council of the Nationalist Government of the Republic of China purchased 11 Beechcraft Model D17Rs, the first two being delivered in September 1937. These were painted in Berry's Non-chalking White with four red crosses applied to signify their medical transport status (Fig. 7-6). This proved not to be a good idea, as the opposing Japanese forces used the crosses to more accurately sight their guns as they were shot down! Later deliveries of the Model D17R to China were finished with a special camouflage paint scheme in green, blue, and brown to help their concealment on the ground and in the air (Fig. 7-7). Five were delivered in the autumn of 1938 (including one in parts for spares) and a further four were delivered in October 1939. Additional aircraft from UC-43 production were delivered under Lend-Lease finished in the regulation Olive Drab paint scheme.

Smithsonian/Beech

7-6 First of a batch of 11 Model D17Rs for the Nationalist Government of the Republic of China. The first two were painted in Berry's Non-chalking White with red crosses. These markings made good ground targets for Japanese fighter planes.

7-7 Later deliveries of Beechcrafts to China used this special blue, green and brown camouflage scheme.

Mr. C.R. "Scotty" Burwood told Robert T. Smith of his experience flying these Beechcrafts when he was personal pilot to the Chinese Nationalist leader, Generalissimo Chiang Kai-shek, who was fighting the Communist Chinese on one side and the Japanese on the other. The speedy Wright-powered Beechcraft proved to be faster than any fighting planes the Japanese had, so Burwood and the Generalissimo were able to keep one step ahead of the advancing forces.

The Brazilian Navy purchased four Beechcraft Model D17A biplanes in 1939, which were used for the Correio Aereo Naval (CAN). This was the Navy's Air Mail Service and was designated as the Postal Aircraft Group of the Southern Routes, flying from Rio de Janeiro to Rio Grande (Fig. 7-8). With the creation of the Ministry of Aeronautics in January 1941, the CAN merged with the Correio Aereo Militar (CAM—Army Air Mail) to form the Correio Aereo Nacional (CAN). It is still in existence today. The Forca Aerea Brasilei received a total of 51 Beechcraft UC-43/GB2, during World War II, including 31 supplied under Lend-Lease. A Model F17D was also impressed into service with the FAB in 1946 from the Brazilian Civil Aviation Department.

British travellers

The British Royal Navy and Royal Air Force received a total of 105 Beechcraft Model D17S aircraft under Lend-Lease, which were designated Traveller Mk.1. The Royal Navy Travellers were flown from the Beech Aircraft factory at Wichita to Fort Dix (now McGuire AFB), where they were dismantled and crated for transport by rail to Newark, New Jersey. Here they were loaded aboard ship for the Atlantic crossing to Great Britain.

Smithsonian/Beech

7-8 Four Beechcraft Model D17R transports were delivered to the Brazilian Navy in 1939 for the Navy's Air Mail Service. Photo shows the third delivered (Be 207).

The 30 Travellers delivered to the Royal Air Force were marked in the serial ranges FL653 to 670 and FZ428 to 439 (Fig. 7-9). These were shipped in batches from New York to Suez in the Middle East in March 1943 aboard the SS *Tabian,* in April 1943 aboard the SS *Agurmonte,* and in October 1943 aboard the SS *Philip Schugler.* Twelve of these aircraft were lost at sea when the SS *Agurmonte* was torpedoed by a German U-boat on May 29, 1943, at position 34.52S 19.33E off Quoin point, Cape Province, South Africa. Recently estimates have been made to assess the possibilities of an undersea search and recovery operation for these crated Beechcrafts, each potentially worth about $250,000. No takers have yet been found.

Wing Commander David Bennett, RAF, has related how at least six of these Travellers served with the Communications Flight at the Royal Air Force base at Khormaksar, in the Aden Protectorate (Fig. 7-10). The Travellers flew missions in the Yemen, in Southern Arabia, and for daily reconnaissance flights along these coastlines looking for signs of any landings by German of Japanese submarine crews on the beaches.

Amongst the 308,567 Allied aircraft ferried by the men and women pilots of the British Air Transport Auxiliary (ATA) during the war were the 75 Beechcraft Travellers delivered to Royal Navy units.

Wartime records for the Royal Navy Travellers in the serial range FT461 to FT535 have not survived, but Air-Britain (Historians) have noted their use with "Stations Flights" at most of the shore-based RN units in the UK as well as serving RN Squadrons in England, Northern Ireland, and Scotland (Fig. 7-11).

7-9 Fresh from the Beech factory, USAAF 310886 also carries the Royal Air Force serial FZ438 on the rear fuselage and the factory serial 4934 on the cowl. Note the star and bar marking outlined in red, dating the picture between June 29 and September 4, 1943. This Traveller was shipped to the Middle East on February 1, 1944, and struck off charge October 27, 1944.

7-10 This Royal Air Force Traveller was flown in the Middle East by Wing Commander David Bennett on communication and reconnaissance missions. FZ432 is shown over the rugged terrain in the Yemen, Southern Arabia, March 1944.

7-11 A Royal Navy Traveller Mk.1 assigned to No. 782 Communication Squadron, based at HMS *Merlin*, Donibristle, Scotland, from June 1944 until September 1945. Note the aircraft radio call sign "Merlin 29" on the forward fuselage.

One of four Beechcrafts impressed into RAF military service during World War II was the USAAC YC-43 flown by Brigadier General Martin F. Scanlon, the Air Attache at the U.S. Embassy in London. This was impressed as DR628 on May 1, 1941 to 24 Squadron RAF, based at Hendon, London. It was used by the Allied Flight and for a time it was flown by Prince Bernhardt, who had escaped from the Netherlands. Later that year, the Prince was to have his own Beechcraft, marked PB-1, which had been delivered to the Netherlands Purchasing Commission on September 20, 1941. After an adventurous career in Southern Rhodesia and South Africa, the YC-43 returned to the United States and is currently airworthy in Bellevue, Washington (N295BS).

The Model C17R (G-AESJ) that had been exhibited at the Brussels Exhibition (and later owned by racing pilot Charles E. Gardner) was sold to the Aeronautical Research & Sales Corporation in April 1939 and based at Heston aerodrome, London. This was the "cover" name for Sydney Cotton's clandestine photographic reconnaissance missions over Germany before the start of the Second World War in September. During World War II, this Beechcraft was impressed into the Royal Air Force as DS180 and was used by No. 41 Group for Air Transport Auxiliary (ATA) flights in support of the deliveries of

Allied aircraft to the operational units in the UK. DS180 was scrapped following an accident in 1944.

Two of the U.S. civilian Beechcrafts impressed in the United States were assigned Royal Air Force serials EB279/280 and were flown by the British Air Commission in Washington, DC. The latter aircraft survives as N114H.

The use of "popular" names for U.S. military aircraft in October 1941 was not widely accepted by the public and was almost totally ignored by those in the armed services. Some sources have noted the spelling of the U.S. military UC-43s as "Traveler," but the British designation is spelled "Traveller." The British Travellers were declared obsolete by the Air Ministry on June 5, 1947.

Other impressments

One of the three Royal Australian Air Force Beechcrafts impressed into wartime service (A39-2) was that used by the U.S. Antarctic Expedition in 1940-41. The speed and range performance capabilities of these aircraft were put to good use as navigation escorts to Curtiss P-40 fighters being ferried across the eastern coast of Austalia to the war zone in New Guinea.

The New Zealand Beechcraft (ZK-AEU) was impressed as NZ573 on September 21, 1939. Based at Hobsonville, Auckland, it served as a comunications and ambulance aircraft. Following a ground-loop accident at Taupo airfield in 1943, the Jacobs R-755-1 engine had to be replaced. Eventually a 220-hp Continental W-670-6A was found and the Beechcraft continued in service until "demobbed" in 1946. It is currently being restored in Australia.

Smaller numbers of Beechcrafts were acquired by the military services in Finland (2), Bolivia (1), Honduras (2), Argentina (4) and Uruguay (1).

The Finnish Beechcraft (BC-1) was that donated by Capt. Otto Thaning during the Winter War of 1938/39; it was later flown in civilian marks as OH-PKA. A postwar UC-43 (BC-2) was used from 1951 as the personal transport of the C-in-C of the Finnish Air force. It was scrapped in 1960, but the remains were purchased in 1970 and used in the restoration of N28WK by Wayne Kerr.

Dr. Samuel Bosch is recorded as handling the Beechcrafts delivered to Argentina, the first being the Model B17L flown by O.J. Whitney on its demonstration flight through South America in 1935–36. This Staggerwing is believed to have been traded for the more powerful Model B17R in 1938. A C17L (R319) followed in 1936 and the only Model E17L (R343) was delivered in December 1937 (Fig. 7-12).

The Beechcraft for Bolivia (B-941-S), believed to be a Model D17R, was noted in transit through France Field, Panama Canal, on April 17, 1941, on delivery to the Fuerza Aerea Nacional Bolivia. It was named *Mariscal de Ayacucho* (Fig. 7-13).

Smithsonian/Beech

7-12 The only Model E17L produced (R343) was delivered to Argentina in December 1937. Colours were Gliddens Pirate Red with silver teardrops.

Museum of Flight

7-13 This Model D17R (B-941-S) was seen at France Field, Panama Canal on April 17, 1941, en route for the Bolivian Air Force.

The Model B17L delivered in 1934 to the Escuela Militor de Aviacion in Honduras and marked "11" was written off in a crash some two years later. It was replaced by a C17R, also marked "11," ordered before it was flown by Louise Thaden and Blanche Noyes to their 1936 victory in the Bendix Air Race. The record-breaking Beechcraft was delivered to Colonel William C. Brooks for the Honduran government, on September 12, 1936. It is believed that this Staggerwing may still exist.

A USAAF UC-43 (S-501) was delivered to the Uruguay Air Force after World War II.

Survivors

With the coming of world peace in 1945, large numbers of U.S. military production and impressed Beechcraft UC-43/GB-2 aircraft were offered and returned to civilian use through the Reconstruction Finance Corporation, a government agency charged with the disposal of wartime assets. In Great Britain, surviving Lend-Lease Travellers were returned to the United States or sold to civilian buyers in Europe.

Of the 765 prewar and World War II production Beechcrafts, records held by the author show that 414 Model 17s were returned to or in use by civilian and military owners worldwide in 1945. An additional 20 Model G17S biplanes were sold new between 1946 and 49.

Prewar totals of Beechcraft Model 17s reported by the Civil Aeronautics Administration were 95 on August 1, 1937, and 163 on January 1, 1939.

The annual *Statistical Study of U.S. Civil Aircraft* dated November 1947 lists a total of 215 Beech Model 17 Staggerwings. This was before all of the war-surplus aircraft had been disposed of by the War Assets Administration. By 1952, the number of active Staggerwings was recorded as 179, but this number declined to 85 in 1969. A worldwide total of 174 "active" Model 17s (i.e., current or on display) was recorded in March 1989.

Census	Active	Inactive	Total
1947			215
1949			322
1950	213	112	325
1951	195	116	311
1952	179	137	316
1955	181	119	300
1958	135	131	266
1963	114	147	261

Census	Active	Inactive	Total
1965	93	162	255
1969	85	171	256
1989	174	85	259

A major reason for this welcome reversal of the number of "active" Beech-craft Model 17s is the interest and expertise offered by the Beech Staggerwing Club and Museum Foundation, located at William Northern Field, Tullahoma, Tennessee, some 60 miles from the birthplace of Walter H. Beech.

Staggerwing club

In keeping with several other classic biplane designs, a suggestion from the Antique Aircraft Association set ex-U.S. Navy pilot and Staggerwing owner Walter C. "Dub" Yarbrough on the road to forming a "type" club. Through this, pilots could exchange their views and experiences in maintaining the numbers of active Beech Model 17s and in assisting each other in the restoration of "inactive" Staggerwings.

The first *Stagger Wing Club Newsletter* dated May 1963 was followed in September 1965 by the first Annual Fly-In and Convention. Eight Staggerwings called in at the Beech Aircraft factory at Wichita enroute to the AAA Meeting at Ottumwa, Iowa. So impressed were the executives of the Beech Aircraft Corporation that Mrs. Olive Ann Beech, President of the Company, hosted later annual meets in 1977, 1982, and 1987. The Staggerwing Club continues under the able direction of President J.C. "Jim" Gorman.

Staggerwing Museum Foundation

Following a suggestion from record-holder Louise Thaden, the Staggerwing Club was able to raise funds to complete the first Staggerwing Museum Foundation building, which was dedicated on June 14, 1974. It comprises the Louise Thaden Office and Library housed in a 100-year old log cabin. The adjoining Walter H. Beech Hangar, completed June 13, 1975, houses several models of the Staggerwing and Travel Air biplanes. The Library contains memorobilia from the flying life of Louise Thaden (including her flying licence, signed by Orville Wright), and the Bendix Trophy won in a Staggerwing in 1936. The two buildings were connected by a lounge in 1979, and house a fine collection of Beech factory, Staggerwing, and Travel Air photographs, data, and drawings, supported by original sketches of Beechcraft Model 17 customer color schemes.

In June 1976, several Beech employees joined together in the Staggerwing Restoration Society to restore the number 231 Model E17B (NC19467) donated to the Museum by Dr. James Scott of Lansing, Michigan. Presided over by Company Archivist Miss Letha Breit, this band of Beechcrafters completed much of the restoration before the components were moved to the Museum Foundation in May 1983 for completion (Fig. 8-1).

To further expand the Museum Foundation, construction began in 1980 of the Olive Ann Beech Gallery and Chapel, which was completed and dedicated June 13, 1981. New ground was broken in June 1983 for the Eddie Ross Staggerwing Restoration Center to provide a facility for the specialist rebuilding and servicing of Travel Air and Beechcraft biplanes. The building was dedicated June 9, 1984, and two ongoing projects are the completion of the Model E17B (NC19467) and the Wright Whirlwind-powered Travel Air "Speedwing" Model D-4000 (NR671H).

In 1983, antique aircraft restorer Steve Pfister, living in Santa Paula, California, researched the fate of the first fixed-gear Beechcraft Model 17 (NC499N). His search led him to the Nunda Chamber of Commerce in New York, where the prototype biplane had crashed in the winter of 1935, and subsequently to the accident site. Amazingly, parts of the airframe were found and sent to Steve, who then sought to acquire the title deed to the Beechcraft from the Ethyl Corporation. This was successful, as was his attempt to recover the original

8-1 Restoration of the Model E17B (NC17083) shows the complex steel tube structure covered with wooden formers and stringers, which made the single-engined Beechcrafts so labor-intensive to build.

CAA license number 499N from the FAA in Oklahoma City.

With original factory drawings from the Museum Foundation, Steve Pfister set about cleaning the recovered parts of the Number One Beechcraft Model 17, manufacturing and adding new parts as required (Fig. 8-2). In May 1985, Steve had progressed far enough to allow news of his project to be published in the Museum's Newsletter, *Media*. Regular updates have kept members advised of progress, and at the time of this writing (March 1989), major fuselage and tail components have been completed, assembled, and covered.

The "survivability" of the sturdy Staggerwing is well shown in the history of the 295th Beechcraft to leave the factory (in June 1939). Built to an order from the United States Army Air Corps (39–139), it was delivered to London and flown by the U.S. Air Attache. It served the Royal Air Force during World War II as DR628, and following its "demobilization" from war service in 1947 was given the U.S. Civil registration NC91397. By 1950, it had been sold to Mrs. Irene Marradya, an English lady living in Colchester (G-AMBY), and the following year was again sold, this time to Commercial Air Services in Southern

8-2 Scale model of the prototype fixed-gear Model 17R (499N) by California restorer Steve Pfister.

Rhodesia (VP-YIV). It remained there until 1972, when it was sold to Mr. P.H. Dahl in Messina, South Africa, as ZS-PWD. Following restoration work in 1978, it finally arrived back in the United States in 1987 and is currently based in Bellevue, Washington (N295BS), resplendent in its original United States Army Air Corps colors!

In 1985, Mr. Yarbrough handed over the office of President of the Staggerwing Museum Foundation to John L. Parish, and took the office of President of the Travel Air Division, where he was able to further the aims of maintaining the earlier aircraft designs overseen by Walter H. Beech. His current project is the restoration of the special Travel Air D-4000 (NR671H) in which Louise Thaden won the 1929 Los Angeles to Cleveland Woman's Air Derby. A 60th anniversary comemorative flight is planned for August 1989, with a commercial DC-9 pilot Susan Desenbury from Greensboro, North Carolina, piloting the restored Travel Air.

8-3 Displayed for all to see in the National Air and Space Museum, Washington, DC, this Model C17B (NC15840) was delivered to Mr. E.E. Aldrin of Standard Oil in July, 1936. It was donated to the Museum by Mr. S. Kavrick.

8-4 One of two Beechcrafts on display in Australia, this Model F17D (VH-ACU) is at the Air World Collection, Wangaratta, New South Wales. It served with the RAAF in WWII as A39-1, navigating Curtiss P-40 fighters to New Guinea.

The Staggerwing Club and Museum Foundation serves more than 350 pilot and enthusiast members of the Travel Air and Beechcraft Model 17 activities worldwide. The 259 Staggerwings on record are located as follows:

United States	236	
Canada	9	
Australia	5	
Great Britain	2	(1 is U.S.-registered)
South Africa	2	
Argentina	1	
Brazil	1	
Germany	2	(U.S.-registered)
Switzerland	1	(U.S.-registered)

Of these, 174 are currently flying or on display, 70 are under restoration, and the remaining 15 are dismantled or stored. A 1988 listing of surviving Staggerwings is shown in Appendix B.

The *Staggerwing Club Newsletters* and *Museum Foundation Media* are a good source of pilot information and restoration material, including such items as replacement wheels, brakes, retract gear motors, and vibrating landing and flying wires. Membership in the Staggerwing Museum Foundation, Inc., is $25 per year and the Staggerwing Club for pilots is $15 per year, from P.O. Box 550, Tullahoma, TN 37388. Copies of the book *Staggerwing* by Robert T. Smith are also available from the Museum Foundation.

8-5 Painted in U.S. Navy markings, this GB-2 (23688) is on display in the hangar deck of the USS *Yorktown* (CV-10) at Patriots Point, Charleston, South Carolina.

8-6 Finished in the Olive Drab colors of the U.S. Army 8th Air Force in England in 1943, this UC-43 (44-76068) is on display at the USAF Museum, Wright-Patterson AFB, Ohio.

Staggerwings on Display

A total of 18 Staggerwings are currently on Display and are located as follows (Figs. 8-3 through 8-7):

B17L	NC270Y	Beech Aircraft Delivery Center, Wichita, Kansas.
B17L	NC15485	Staggerwing Museum Foundation, Tullahoma, Tennessee.
C17B	NC15840	National Air and Space Museum, Washington, D.C.
C17B	N962W	Staggerwing Museum Foundation, Tullahoma, Tennessee.
GB-2	*CF-BKQ	Reynolds Museum, Wetaskiwin, Alberta, Canada.
D17S	N1178V	U.S. Naval Aviation Museum, Pensacola, Florida.
D17S	N1336V	Planes of Fame East Air Museum, Eden Prairie, Minnesota.
D17S	N20753	Staggerwing Museum Foundation, Tullahoma, Tennessee.
D17S	N278WW	Wedell-Williams Memorial, Patterson, Louisiana.
D17S	N4512N	Lone Star Flight Museum, Houston, Texas.
D17S	N51746	Yankee Air Corps, Chino, California.
D17S	N67735	Weeks Air Museum, Miami, Florida.
D17S	VH-BBL	Joe Drage, Air World, Wangaratta, Australia.
E17B	*NC19467	Staggerwing Museum Foundation, Tallahoma, Tennessee.
F17D	N20798	Staggerwing Museum Foundation, Tullahoma, Tennessee.
F17D	VH-ACU	Joe Drage, Air World, Wangaratta, Australia.
G17S	N44G	John L. Parish, Tullahoma, Tennessee.
GB-2	Bu23688	USS *Yorktown* Memorial, Charleston, South Carolina.
UC-43	44-76068	USAF Museum, Wright-Patterson AFB, Ohio.
UC-43	FAB2778	Aerospace Museum, Rio de Janeiro, Brazil.

*Stored, awaiting restoration.

8-7   Finished in wartime U.S. Navy colors, this GB-2 (N1336V) is on display at the Planes of Fame East Air Museum, Eden Prarie, Minnesota.

Flying
the
Staggerwing

Staggerwing Foundation President John Parish took me for a flight in his Model G17S in October 1988. I followed him through the ground, taxiing, and flight checks.

Preflighting the Staggerwing is routine, but add special checks on the flying and landing wires, main undercarriage, and fabric covering. Both front seats must be occupied if three or more persons are aboard, but watch your head on the V struts if you sit up front. There is a good view above, below, and to the side, but the tail-down attitudes on the ground and large cowl limit forward visibility. The "air" of a prewar automobile is strongly felt. Engine start is routine for the Wasp Junior—fuel pump, throttle, "clear prop," and starter button (Fig. 9-1). (A pilot checklist is in appendix G.)

Taxiing is not straightforward due to the large radial engine up front, but a weaving side-to-side scan or safety pilot in the right-hand seat will get you to the takeoff point. On the engine run-up, exercise the prop twice and complete the trim, mixture, prop, fuel, and flap checks.

One word of warning: Keep an eye on the fuel pressure gauge and fully understand the arrangements for managing the fuel tanks, up to a total of six—four wing plus front and rear fuselage tanks. The upper and lower selector fuelcocks are on the lower right of the front panel and should be clearly placarded. Take off and land using the main tank; then, in sequence, use the left upper, right upper, left lower, and right lower wing tanks.

Taxi onto the runway, line up, lock the tailwheel, and open the throttle smoothly to 36 inches and 2300 rpm. Keep straight with the rudder and allow the tail to come up naturally. Around 80 mph, ease the Staggerwing into the air, brake the wheels, and raise the gear. Climb out at 100 mph, reducing power to 29 inches. On reaching cruising altitude, set 27 inches at 2000 rpm. At 10,000 feet, a clean Staggerwing will record 200 mph at 65 percent power. Depending on the fuel load, up to three passengers may share the rear bench seat, and they enjoy a comfortable ride.

From the copilot's seat, I found the inflight visibility outstanding for a biplane. You sit well forward and the view is similar to that of the low-wing Grummans and Pipers I usually fly. I liked the wind-down side windows, just like a car! Many Staggerwings have real comfort for pilots and passengers built into the cabin.

The Staggerwing feels extremely stable in flight and did not respond to mild turbulence. The controls are firm and instrument flight is reported to be a pleasant experience. When trimmed for cruise, rate one turns will continue hands-off.

9-1 Updated instrument panel of the Model G17S N44G. A stable platform in IFR weather conditions, the Staggerwing is a delight to fly.

Stalls are unusual (and occur at 65 mph flaps and gear up, 60 mph flaps and gear down). The lower wing appears to stall first (some believe the incidence is set slightly higher, but Beech manuals do not confirm this) and the center of lift moves quickly aft, lowering the nose, even if the controls are held back. If this condition is maintained, the lower wing begins to fly again, thus causing the nose to come up until the lower wing again stalls and the process is repeated. Thus the aircraft will oscillate gently up and down, meanwhile slowly losing altitude (Fig. 9-2).

This oscillating stall, coupled with noseheaviness, explains why three-point landings can be demanding. If the wheels are not just inches off the runway approaching touchdown and the lower wing stalls, the nose goes down and a mainwheel-first landing occurs. The resulting bounce is best recovered by a go-around.

Reduce the airspeed to not more than 100 mph entering the landing pattern. Check that the fuel is selected to the main tank and that the brakes are off. Keep an eye on the fuel pressure gauge. Lower the landing gear, set the mixture rich and carb heat cold, prop to fine, set half flap and trim. Set up the final approach at 90 mph with full flap and aim to cross the runway threshold at 80 mph.

Experiencing and later watching the many Staggerwing landings at Wichita and Tullahoma, many pilots complete mainwheel landings and keep the tail high

9-2 From any angle, the sight of a Beechcraft Staggerwing is unique. This Model G17S (N44G) is flown by its proud owner, John L. Parish.

until rudder control is being lost, when directional control is continued with wheel brakes. Full-stall taildown landings can be made, but they need that extra judgement and care.

During the landing roll, full rudder may be required to keep straight; as speed slows, prompt and firm use of the brakes will keep you on the centerline. Unlock the tailwheel, raise the flaps and resume a weaving side-to-side scan taxiing in.

Once you have parked, shut down the engine and switch off the systems, chock the wheels and tie everything down. Take another look at the Beechcraft as you leave and note that sensuous curve of the fin and rudder, the finely sculpted wingtips, the crackling heat from beneath the cowling, and you'll walk away with that satisfied "Staggerwing smile."

10

Building your own

Models

At least two flying models and one plastic kit of the Staggerwing are available from:

BYRON ORIGINALS, INC.
P.O. Box 279, Ida Grove, Iowa 51445
77-inch, 1/5th scale flying model

ROYAL PRODUCTS CORP.
790 W. Tennessee Ave., Denver, Colorado 80223
56-inch span flying model

STAGGERWING UNLIMITED
19 Immelman St., Hampshire, Illinois 60140
1/32nd scale plastic kit.

Model plans are also available from:

THE AEROMODELLER PLANS SERVICE (G.A.G. Cox; July 1963)
9 Hall Rd., Maylands Wood Estate, Hemel Hempstead,
Herts, England HP2 7BH
Model D17S and G17S (Fig. 10-1 on pages 106 and 107).

R/C Modeler Magazine
144 W. Sierra Blvd., P.O. Box 487, Sierra Madre, California 91024
Model G17S; December 1975

FLYING MODELS (Bryce Peterson; July 1967)
215 Park Ave. South, New York, New York 10003
Model G17S

Model Airplane News (Budd Davisson; November 1987)
632 Danbury Rd., Wilton, Connecticut 06897
W.A. Wylam, all Model 17s

CLEVELAND MODEL & SUPPLY CO. (Edward T. Packard)
10307R Detroit Ave., Cleveland, Ohio 44102
Model C17B

Homebuilts

Several experimental homebuilt designs featuring the negative-stagger wing arrangement have been successfully flown and plans are available.

The Sorrell SNS-7 Hiperbipe is the negative-stagger tailwheel design from Hobert C. Sorrell; it won the EAA "Outstanding New Design" award in 1973. Sorrell's first designs in 1963 were powered by small 18-hp golf-cart engines, but the current aerobatic two-seat model uses a 180-hp Lycoming O-360-B1E. With a wingspan of 22 feet 10 inches and a gross weight of 1,911 pounds, the Hiperbipe cruises at 160 mph for 500 miles.

For the ultralight aviator, Sorrell has also flown the SNS-9 EXP. II, a two-seat tailwheel design powered by a 42-hp Rotax engine, with a wingspan of 23 feet 4 inches and a gross weight of 810 pounds.

Homebuilt kits and plans are available from:

SORRELL AVIATION
16525 Tilley Rd., Tenino, Washington 98589

Of a similar layout but with nosewheel gear is William H. Durand's Mk.V, first flown in 1978. Powered by a 150-hp Lycoming O-320-E2A, wing span is 24 feet 6 inches and gross weight is 1,840 pounds. The Durand Mk.V cruises at 125 mph for 400 miles.

Plans are available from

DURAND ASSOCIATES INC.
84th and McKinley Rd., Omaha, Nebraska 68122.

Across the border in Canada, Lou Hansen of Langley, British Columbia, finished another tailwheel negative-stagger design, the "Shaunee," in August 1987 (Fig. 10-2 on page 108). Power is from a 150-hp Lycoming O-320.

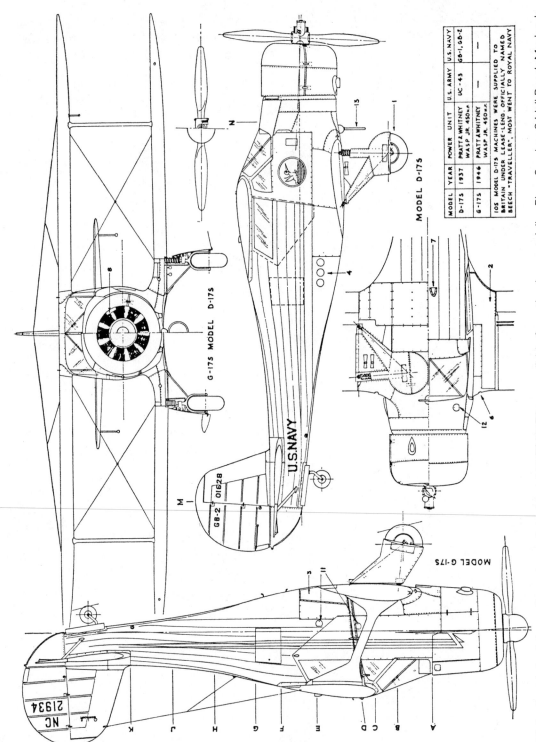

MODEL	YEAR	POWER UNIT	U.S. ARMY	U.S. NAVY
D-17S	1937	PRATT & WHITNEY WASP JR. 450 H.P.	UC-43	GB-1, GB-2
G-17S	1946	PRATT & WHITNEY WASP JR. 450 H.P.	—	—

105 MODEL D-17S MACHINES WERE SUPPLIED TO BRITAIN UNDER LEASE-LEND. OFFICIALLY NAMED BEECH "TRAVELLER", MOST WENT TO ROYAL NAVY

10-1 Reprints of these three-views of the Model D17S/G17S are available from the Aeromodeller Plans Service, 9 Hall Road, Maylands Wood Estate, Hemel Hempstead, England, HP2 7BH.

(ARGUS SPECIALIST PUBLICATIONS)

DRAWN BY G.A.G. COX.

U.S. Navy GB-2 : All silver, black lettering.
G-17S NC21934 : All white with registration,
fuselage trim and front 4 in.
of cowl in red. Narrow gold
pinstripe round all red areas.
Wing walk and scuff plate black.

Emblem of N.A.S. Pensacola : White goose with
yellow beak and feet. Brown
helmet, light blue sky, blue-
green and white water, red
border.

MODEL G-17S

Reprints of this 1/48th scale plan and dyeline prints of the 1/36th
scale original are available as plan pack AF2770 price 2/6d. plus
6d. post from the Aeromodeller Plans Service.

FT.

Notes

1. Undercarriage mechanically identical on both
models. Shown on load G-17S, off load D-17S.
2. Wing walk. 3. Scuff plate. 4. Flare tubes.
5. Venturi on port side. 6. Cabin air intake.
7. Cabin ventilator. 8. Carburettor intake.
9. Metal panel over fuel tanks. 10. Ply panel.-
11. Fuel fill access. 12. Oil fill access. 13. D/F
loop on military machines only. 14. Location of
insignia, GB-2.

BEECHCRAFT D-17S AND G-17S

Building Your Own 107

10-2 The negative-stagger layout has not had many followers, but this homebuilt "Shaunee" (C-GSDH) by Lou Hansen was seen at Langley, British Columbia, in August 1987.

Specifications

Following the first model, only the variations in weight or performance are noted.

Model 17R—ATC.496   December 20, 1932—2 Built
Engine: Wright R-975-E2 Whirlwind 9-cylinder radial
Power: 420 hp @ 2,200 rpm; 80-octane fuel
Fuel: 115–145 U.S. gals
Consumption: 24 gal/hr
Still air range: 840–1050 miles
Span: 34 ft 4 in
Length: 24 ft 3 in
Height: 8 ft 8 in
Wing area: 323 sq ft (includes half area of fuselage)
Gross weight: 4,500 lbs
Empty weight: 2,700 lbs
Wing loading: 13.93 lb/sq ft
Power loading: 10.71 lb/hp
Max speed: 201 mph
Cruise: 170 mph
Land: 60 mph
Climb: 1,500 ft/min
Ceiling: 20,000 ft
Features:
    Ailerons: Lower
    Split rudder (Later modified with drag flaps)
    Wire-braced tail
    Narrow-track, fixed panted gear

Fixed tailwheel
Adjustable tailplane

Model A17F—ATC.548—August 8, 1934—1 Built

Engine: Wright R-1820-F11 9-cylinder radial
Power: 690 hp @ 1,950 rpm; 87-octane fuel
Fuel: 155 gals
Consumption: 40 U.S. gals/hr
Still air range: 820 miles
Span: 34 ft 6 in
Length: 24 ft 3 in
Height: 8 ft 10 in
Wing area: 305 sq ft
Gross weight: 5,200 lbs
Empty weight: 3,285 lbs
Wing loading: 14.6 lb/sq ft
Power loading: 7.73 lb/hp
Max speed: 235 mph
Cruise: 212 mph @ 80 percent
Climb: 2,500 ft/min
Ceiling: 25,000 ft
Features:
    Airlerons: Lower
    Drag flaps: Upper
    Strut-Braced Tail
    Wide-track, fixed panted gear
    Swivelling tailwheel
    Rudder and elevator tab

Model A17FS—ATC. 577—July 6, 1935—1 Built

Engine: Wright SR-1820-F3 Cyclone 9-cylinder radial
Power: 710 hp @ 1,950 rpm
Wing area: 338 sq ft (including half the fuselage)
Gross weight: 6,000 lbs
Max speed: 235 mph
Cruise: 215 mph @ 5,000 ft
Climb: 2,000 ft/min
Ceiling: 20,000 ft
Features: As A17F

Model B17L—ATC.560—December 4, 1934—46 Built

Engine: Jacobs L-4 (R-775-D) 7-cylinder radial
Power: 225 hp @ 2,000 rpm; 175 hp @ 1,900 rpm
Fuel: 50–120 U.S. gallons; 73-octane; 13.2 gal/hr
Propeller: 7 ft 6 in diameter wooden Hartzell fixed pitch
    (or a fixed metal Curtiss or a controllable Lycoming Smith)
Still Air Range: 600–1,470 miles
Seats: 4 to 5; with three passengers on rear seat, only 75 lbs of baggage allowed
Span: 32 ft
Length: 24 ft 5 in
Height: 8 ft 6 in
Wing area: 273 sq ft
Gross weight: 3,150–3,165 lbs
Empty weight: 1,650 lbs
Seaplane: 3,525 lbs (Edo 38-3430 floats)
Wing loading: 11.53 lb/sq ft
Power loading: 14 lb/hp
Top speed: 175 mph @ SL
Cruise: 162 mph @ 5,000 ft
Flaps: 115 mph
Land: 45 mph
Climb: 1,000 ft/min
Ceiling: 15,000 ft
Features:
    Ailerons: Lower
    Drag flaps: Lower
    Strut-braced tail
    Long u/c
    No tailwheel doors
    Rib spacing: 7.5 inches

Model B17B—ATC.560—December 4, 1934—1 Built

Engine: Jacobs L-5 (R-830-1) 7-cylinder radial
Power: 285 hp @ 2,000 rpm; 17.5 gal/hr; 7 ft 9 in Curtiss propeller
Still air range: 505–1,210 miles
Top Speed: 185 mph @ SL
Cruise: 177 mph @ 7,200 ft
Climb: 1,100 ft/min
Ceiling: 18,000 ft
Features: As B17L

Model B17E—ATC.566—May 9, 1935—4 Built

Engine: Wright R-760-E1, 7-cylinder radial
Power: 285 hp @ 2100 rpm; 17.5 gal/hr; 7 ft 6 in Curtiss propeller
Span: 32 ft
Length: 24 ft 5 in
Height: 8 ft 2 in
Wing area: 267 sq ft
Gross weight: 3,263–3,615 lbs
Empty weight: 2,000 lbs
Climb: 1,200 ft/min
Cruise: 177 @ 7,200 ft
Features:
    Ailerons: Lower
    Drag flaps: Upper
    Strut-braced tail
    Short u/c
    Different wingtip shape

Model B17R—ATC.579—July 22, 1935—15 Built

Engine: Wright R-975-E2, 9-cylinder radial
Power: 420 hp @ 2,200 rpm; 7 ft 3 in Curtiss propeller
Fuel: 70–170 gal
Gross weight: 3,600–3615 lbs
Empty weight: 2,238 lbs
Seaplane: 3,972 lbs (Edo 39-4000 floats)
Wing area: 267 sq ft
Climb: 1,400 ft/min
Cruise: 202 mph @ 9,000 ft
Flaps: 100 mph
Land: 50 mph
Features: As B17E

Model C17B—ATC.602—April 16, 1936—39 Built

Engine: Jacobs L-5/5M/5MB (R-830-1), 7-cylinder radial
Power: 285 hp @ 2,000 rpm; 7 ft 9 in Curtiss fixed metal propeller
Fuel: 74–166 gals; 17.5 gal/hr
Gross weight: 3,150–3,165 lbs
Amphibian: 3,525 lbs (Edo 49–3875 floats)
Span: 32 ft
Length: 24 ft 5 in

Height: 8 ft 2 in
Wing area: 273 sq ft
Climb: 1,100 ft/min
Cruise: 177 mph @ 7,200 ft
Land: 45 mph
Features:
    Ailerons: Lower
    Drag flaps: Lower
    Strut-braced tail
    Short u/c
    No tailwheel doors
    Rib spacing 8.5 inches
    Angle of incidence changed on horizontal stabilizer

Model C17L—ATC.602—April 16, 1936—6 Built

Engine: Jacobs L-4/4MA/4MB (R-755-D), 7-cylinder radial
Power: 225 hp @ 2,000 rpm; 14 gal/hr; 7 ft 6 in Hartzell propeller
Climb: 850 ft/min
Cruise: 166 mph @ 7,200 ft
Features: As C17B

Model C17R—ATC.604—May 6, 1936—17 Built

Engine: Wright R-975-E2 Whirlwind, 9-cylinder radial
Power: 420 hp @ 2,200 rpm; 8 ft 3 in Curtiss metal fixed propeller
Fuel: 98–173 gals
Gross weight: 3,900–3,915 lbs
Seaplane: 4,105 lbs (Edo 39–4000 floats)
Climb: 1,400 ft/min
Cruise: 202 mph @ 10,000 ft
Features:
    Ailerons: Lower
    Drag flaps: Upper

Model C17E—ATC.615—July, 1936—2 Built

Engine: Wright R-760-E1 Whirlwind, 7-cylinder radial
Power: 285 hp @ 2,100 rpm; 7 ft 6 in Curtiss metal fixed propeller
Gross weight: 3,600–3,615 lbs
Climb: 1,200 ft/min
Cruise: 177 @ 7,200 ft
Features: As C17R

Model D17R—ATC.638—May 20, 1937—26 Built

Engine: Wright R-975-E3 (R-975-11) Whirlwind 9-cylinder
Power: 450 hp @ 2,250 rpm; Hamilton-Standard propeller
Fuel: 102–174 U.S. gals; 80 octane; 23 gal/hr
Still air range: 875–1,495 miles
Span: 32 ft
Length: 26 ft 11 in
Height: 8 ft 0 in
Wing area: 296 sq ft
Gross weight: 4,200–4,250 lbs
Empty weight: 2,460 lbs
Seaplanes; 4,600 lbs
Max Speed: 211 mph @ SL
Cruise: 202 mph @ 9.700 ft
Climb: 1,400 ft/min
Ceiling: 24,000 ft
Flaps: 115 mph
Land: 50 mph
Features:
    Ailerons: Upper
    Plain flaps: Lower
    Cantilever tail
    Short u/c
    Tailwheel doors
    Rib spacing: 6.5 inches
    Long fuselage

Model D17S—ATC.649—July 16, 1937—68 Built

Engine: Pratt & Whitney R-985-SB Wasp Junior 9-cylinder
Power: 450 hp @ 2,300 rpm; 8 ft 3 in Hamilton-Standard propeller
Span: 32 ft
Length: 25 ft 11 in
Height: 8 ft 0 in
Max speed: 212 @ SL
Cruise: 202 mph @ 9,700 ft
Climb: 1,400 ft/min
Ceiling: 26,000 ft
Features:
    Toe brakes
    New windscreen
    Reinforced wingtips

Model D17A—ATC.713—November 7, 1939—8 Built
Engine: Wright R-760-E3 Whirlwind 7-cylinder
Power: 350 hp @ 2,400 rpm; Hamilton-Standard propeller
Fuel: 98–170 gals; 80 octane; 17.5 gal/hr
Span: 32 ft
Length: 26 ft 8 in
Height: 8 ft 0 in
Max speed: 180 mph @ SL
Cruise: 180 mph @ 9,600 ft
Climb: 800 ft/min
Ceiling: 17,000 ft
Features: As D17S

Model D17W—No ATC—2 Built
Engine: Pratt & Whitney R-985-SC-G Wasp Junior 9-cylinder
Power: 600 hp @ 2,850 rpm
Fuel: 79-121 gals; 87 octane, 29 gal/hr
Span: 32 ft
Length: 27 ft 0 in
Height: 8 ft 0 in
Gross weight: 4,200 lbs
Empty: 2,800 lbs
Max speed: 235 mph @ 13,500 ft
Cruise: 225 mph at 13,500 ft
Climb: 2,400 ft/min
Ceiling: 30,000 ft
Features: As D17S

Model E17B—ATC.641—May 22, 1937—54 Built
Engine: Jacobs L-5 (R-830-1) 7-cylinder radial
Power: 285hp @ 2,000 rpm; 7 ft 9 in Curtiss-Reed propeller
Fuel: 77–125 U.S. gallons; 73 octane; 16.8 gal/hr
Still Air Range: 810–1,315 miles.
Span: 32 ft
Length: 25 ft 11 in
Height: 8 ft
Wing area: 296 sq ft
Gross weight: 3,350–3,390 lbs
Empty weight: 2,080 lbs
Seaplane: 3,700 lbs (Edo 39–4000 floats)

Wing loading: 11.32 lb/sq ft
Power loading: 11.75 lb/hp
Top speed: 185 mph @ SL
Cruise: 177 mph @ 7,200 ft
Flaps: 115 mph
Land: 45 mph
Climb: 1,200 ft/min
Ceiling: 18,000 ft
Features:
    Ailerons: Upper
    Plain flaps: Lower
    Strut-braced tail
    Short u/c
    No tailwheel doors
    Rib spacing: 8 inches

Model E17L—ATC.641—May 22, 1937—1 Built

Engine: Jacobs L-4 (R-755-D) 7-cylinder
Power: 225 hp @ 2,000 rpm
Fuel: 34–64 gals; 14 gal/hr
Climb: 1,000 ft/min
Cruise: 166 mph @ 7,200 ft
Features: As E17B

Model F17D—ATC.689—August 26, 1938—60 Built

Engine: Jacobs L-6/6M/6MB (R-915-A3) 7-cylinder
Power: 330 hp @ 2,200 rpm; 8 ft Curtiss-Reed propeller
Fuel: 77–125 gals; 80 octane; 17 gal/hr
Gross weight: 3,550–3,590 lbs
Seaplane: 3,940 lbs (Edo 39–4000 floats)
Span: 32 ft
Length: 25 ft 11 in
Height: 8 ft 0 in
Climb: 1,300 ft/in
Cruise: 182 mph @ 10,000 ft
Flaps: 117 mph
Land: 46 mph
Features:
    Ailerons: Upper
    Plain flaps: Lower
    Braced tail

Short u/c
Tailwheel doors
Rib spacing: 8 inches

Model G17S—ATC.779—October 11, 1946—20 Built

Engine: Pratt & Whitney R-985-AN1/3/4 Wasp Junior 9-cyl
Power: 450 hp @ 2,300 rpm; 400 hp @ 2,200 rpm @ 5,000 ft
Fuel: 124–170 U.S. gallons; 87 octane
Propeller: Hamilton-Standard constant speed
Consumption: 24.9 U.S. gals/hr
Still air range: 1,000–1,370 miles
Span: 32 ft
Length: 26 ft 9 in
Height: 8 ft
Wing area: 296 sq ft
Gross weight: 4,250 lbs
Empty weight: 2,800 lbs
Wing loading: 14.34 lb/sq ft
Power loading: 9.44 lb/hp
Top speed: 212 @ 5,500 ft mph
Cruise: 201 mph @ 10,000 ft
Flaps: 115 mph
Land: 64 mph
Climb: 1,250 ft/min
Ceiling: 20,000 ft
Features:
    Ailerons: Upper
    Plain flaps: Lower
    Cantilever tail
    Short u/c
    Tailwheel doors
    Rib spacing: 8 inches
    New cowl, fin, and rudder outline, undercarriage doors

Survivors
by Country Registration
as of December 31, 1988

	Registration	Model	Registered Owner
c	C-FGKY	D17S-4874	*Don Saunders, St. Albert, Alberta, Canada
s	CF-BJD	D17S-201	*Ron E. Uloth, Dorothee, Quebec, Canada
r	CF-BKQ	GB-2-4849	Reynolds Museum, Wetaskiwin, Alberta, Canada
c	CF-CCA	D17S-203	*M. Servos, Burlington, Ontario, Canada
c	CF-DTE	D17S-403	*Borje Molin, Wetaskiwin, Alberta, Canada
r	CF-EKA	D17S-4813	*Ron E. Uloth, Dorothee, Quebec, Canada
r	CF-GKW	C17R-120	*Bill Boucock, Cochrane, Alberta, Canada
c	CF-GWL	D17S-4870	*George Le May, Calgary, Canada
r	(C-GXQN)	D17S-355	Harry Sorenson, Yellowknife, NW Territories
d	FAB2778	D17S-6691	Aerospace Museum, Rio de Janeiro, Brazil
c	G-BDGK	D17S-4920	*Philip Wolf, Redhill, England
r	LV-XFN	D17S-6915	*Guido A. Jontza, San Lorenzo, Argentina
c	NC1030	D17S-409	*Norman L. Coffelt, Lebanon, OR
r	N1112M	D17S-6684	*John J. Hanusin, Northbrook, IL
c	N1120V	D17S-6734	(Sale reported)
c	N1126V	D17S-6738	*Vern E. Hongola, Manhattan Beach, CA
r	N113Q	D17S-4815	(Sale reported) Peter Bottome, Miami, FL
c	N114H	D17S-327	*Robert A. Hoff, Idaho Falls, IN
r	N115A	F17D-275	*Bennie J. Keltz, Rosedale, IN
c	N1174V	D17S-6892	*John Mihalka, Carson City, NV
d	N1178V	D17S-6917	Carl Thomas, Coconut Grove, FL

---

* = Staggerwing Club member. r = Restoration. d = Display.

c = Current. p = Parts. s = Stored. m = Dismantled.

	Registration	Model	Registered Owner
c	N117DS	D17S-3109	*Raymond Dieckman, Irvine, CA
c	N1180V	D17S-6904	*Nolan F. Carter, El Paso, TX
r	N1181V	D17S-6706	*Victor M. Schmidt, Corbett, OR
c	N1184V	D17S-6748	Overturf Electric Motors, Inc., Columbus, NB
c	N1185V	D17S-6746	*Russell R. Latta, Atwater, CA
c	N1192V	D17S-6884	*Victor M. Schmidt, Corbett, OR
c	N1193V	D17S-6701	Preston Motors, Inc., Kingwood, WV
c	N1195V	D17S-6749	*Douglas R. Womack, Iola, KS
r	N1196V	D17S-6703	*Tom F. Hillier, Escalon, CA
c	N120V	D17S-6734	(Sale reported)
c	N1213V	D17S-1016	*Thomas H. Todd Jr., Memphis, TN
c	N1254N	D17S-1029	*Lloyd H. Cohoon, Bishop, CA
c	N1255N	D17S-4829	*Bill Dause, Wellington, UT
c	N1256B	D17S-4858	*Samuel S. Sewell III, Renton, WA
r	N12589	B17L-7	Howell D. Martin, Wichita, KS
c	N12590	B17L-8	*Salvatore V. Lentine, Ringoes, NJ
r	N12592	B17L-12	*William P. Six, Riverside, CA
c	N127J	F17D-272	*W.D. Montgomery, Williamson, GA
d	N1336V	D17S-6897	Robert J. Trustee-Pond, Plymouth, MN
c	N1341V	D17S-6728	*Jack Haswell, Tifton, GA
c	N139KP	F17D-257	*Peachey & Peachey Farms, Hugoton, KS
r	N14409	B17L-21	*John C. Collins, Newark, CA
r	N14413	B17R-38	Crow Executive Air Charter, Millbury, OH
m	N14415	B17L-28	*Christine M. St. Onge, Wexford, PA
c	N14417	B17L-30	*Thomas R. Rench, Racine, WI
r	N14453	B17L-32	Ellis A. Hallaman, Lebanon, OR
r	N14458	B17E-49	*Chris Kidder, North Syracuse, NY
r	N1532M	D17S-3108	Kenneth R. Mullins, Belleville, MI
r	N15407	B17L-45	*Hubbard Johnson, Red Bluff, CA
d	N15485	B17L-58	*Straggerwing Foundation, Tullahoma, TN
p	N15487	C17R-73	*Chad Norbert Koppie, Gilberts, IL
r	N15815	B17R-70	James Kimball, Zellwood, FL
d	N15840	C17B-93	*National Air and Space Museum, Washington, DC
c	N15846	C17L-89	*Charles O. Kanaga, Wichita, KS
c	N160	D17S-4836	*Arnold D. Widmer, Crete, ND
r	N161K	D17S-4821	*Jim R. Porter, Chicago, IL
c	N16444	C17L-103	*Bruce J. Dexter, Orange, MA
c	N16M	D17S-6765	Chris Jacobson, Arvada, CO
c	N16S	D17S-6687	*Richard Gibson, Rockford, IL

---

* = Staggerwing Club member. r = Restoration. d = Display.

c = Current. p = Parts. s = Stored. m = Dismantled.

	Registration	Model	Registered Owner
r	N17061	C17B-112	Robert M. Schow, Golden, CO
r	N17064	C17B-128	Jim Carrigan, San Jose, CA
r	N17071	E17B-156	*John D. Hoff, Idaho Falls, ID
s	N17072	C17B-130	*Tom Switzer, Baltimore, OH
p	N17073	C17B-131	(Sale reported)
c	N17074	C17B-132	*William A. Hellsel, Seattle, WA
c	N17078	C17B-133	*Bill E. White, Boring, OR
r	N17083	E17B-138	*Staggerwing Foundation, Tullahoma, TN
c	N17643	D17S-4827	*Robert W. Henley, Denver, CO
r	N17679	D17S-6911	*R.R. Fuchs, O'Ffalon, MO
c	N17CV	D17S-4893	R.E. Hale-Julian, Jr., San Francisco, CA
c	N17GB	D17S-4818	*Jess E. Shryack, Decatur, TX
c	N17SF	D17S-6890	*Clancy Haun Flanagan, Chowchilla, CA
c	N17SW	D17S-4850	*James C. Gorman, Mansfield, OH
c	N18028	D17S-147	Leyvan Inc., West Chicago, IL
c	N18555	E17D-157	John M. Schleich, Oceanside, NY
r	N18560	E17B-162	Herman Strafuss, Manhattan, KS
r	N18561	SE17D-210	*James A. Brennen, Beaver, PA
c	N18570	E17B-228	*Robert A. Strasshofer, Homestead, FL
r	N18575	D17S-179	*Willice D. Hill, Justin, TX
c	N18577	E17B-195	Mark A. Peterik, Lafayette, LA
c	N18777	D17S-200	*James W. Alford, Las Vegas, NV
r	N18779	D17S-202	Joseph Erale, Brentwood, New York, NY
r	N18781	E17B-204	*Shirley A. Morrison, Hawthorne, CA
c	N18785	E17B-208	*David L. Oaks, Bellbrook, OH
c	N18BJ	D17S-4891	*Bert Jenson, Crystal Bay, NV
c	N18V	D17S-6869	*Robert Lamplough, Duxford, England
c	N192H	D17S-6723	*Lewis M. Lindemer, Seeley Lake, MT
r	N1944B	D17S-6926	*Charles A. Dogherty, San Antonio, TX
c	N19466	F17D-230	Malcolm A. Soare, Sidney, MT
r	N19467	E17B-231	*Staggerwing Foundation, Tullahoma, TN
c	N19473	F17D-245	*George S. York, Mansfield, OH
p	N19474	F17D-246	(Sale reported)
c	N19482	D17S-254	*Steven J. Craig, Lawrence, KS
c	N19493	D17S-263	*Phillip Ray, Arlington, TX
d	N20753	D17S-395	*Staggerwing Museum Foundation, Tullahoma, TN
c	N20779	D17S-398	*Lloyd H. Cizek, Deronda, WI
d	N20798	F17D-333	*Staggerwing Foundation, Tullahoma, TN
c	N217SD	D17S-3098	Skyhigh Avn. Inc., Vero Beach, FL

* = Staggerwing Club member. r = Restoration. d = Display.

c = Current. p = Parts. s = Stored. m = Dismantled.

	Registration	Model	Registered Owner
c	N2277Z	D17S-4902	*Mike Udall, Eager, AZ
c	N230	D17S-4835	*Frank M. Drendell, Hickory, NC
r	N233EB	E17B-233	*Charles D. Hamilton, Portland, OR
c	N236E	D17S-3179	*Stephen Cooper, Fairbanks, Alaska
r	N239E	D17S-4916	Sydney R. Norris, Whitehouse, NJ
c	N241K	D17S-287	*John Latta, Gustine, CA
c	N2422	D17S-304	*Cynthia A. Jones, Anchorage, AK
c	N248E	D17S-6871	Larry J. Kruljac, Riverside, CA
r	N25K	D17S-6881	*John K. Desmond Jr., Philadelphia, PA
r	N2626	F17D-283	*Jerry Weiler, Port Angeles, WA
c	N264E	D17S-4888	*Denzell W. Marshall, Pasadena, CA
c	N265E	D17S-4940	Morris J. Moriarty, Rye, NH
c	N2663	F17D-330	(Sale reported) Vero Beach, FL
d	N270Y	B17L-3	*Beech Aircraft Corp., Wichita KS
d	N278WW	D17S-264	Weddell Williams Memorial, Patterson, LA
c	N27E	D17S-6883	*George H. Smith, Reading, PA
c	N2801	F17D-392	*W.S. Wallin, Kent, WA
c	N282Y	C17R-75	(Sale reported)
c	N2832D	D17S-1025	*Theodore A. Giltner, Tamaqua, PA
s	NC284Y	E17B-206	*Harry F. Wells, Little River, SC
c	N285D	F17D-256	(Sale reported) Ken Willems, Las Vegas, NV
c	N28A	D17S-6760	Gordon B. Warren, Gunnison, CO
c	N28WK	D17S-4872	*Wayne H. Kerr, Stockton, CA
c	N295BS	D17S-295	*Bruce R. McCaw, Bellevue, WA
r	N322H	D17S-3184	Smitty's Aircraft Service, Inc., O'Neill, NB
r	N333E	D17S-4878	*Selmer A. Thomas, New Castle, CO
c	N34R	G17S-424	(Sale reported) Las Vegas, NV
r	N35E	D17R-167	*Walter B. Thomas Jr., Pilot Mountain, NC
c	N35JM	D17S-6914	*Jack H. Munroe, Denver, CO
c	N368	D17S-4883	Fly M. Hunting Club, Inc., Yerington, NV
r	N39392	D17S-6875	*John L. Harbour, Central Point, OR
c	N40E	D17S-6685	*Glen L. McNabb, Jasper, TN
c	N41663	E17B-196	Brennand Aircraft Sales, Neenah, WI
r	N41852	E17L-160	*Arthur H. McEwen Jr., Daytona Beach, FL
c	N419J	D17S-419	*William D. Carlson, Irvine, CA
m	N420E	D17S-6671	*Edwin R. Walker, Edinburg, TX
r	N44561	D17S-6922	*Charles C. Spencer, Grass Valley, CA
c	N44562	D17S-6923	*Richard W. Hansen, Batavia, IL
d	N44G	G17S-B-3	*John L. Parish, Tullahoma, TN

* = Staggerwing Club member. r = Restoration. d = Display.

c = Current. p = Parts. s = Stored. m = Dismantled.

	Registration	Model	Registered Owner
r	N44GM	D17S-6916	*Lewis W. Lindemer, Seeley Lake, MT
d	N4512N	D17S-6737	Lone Star Flight Museum, Houston, TX
c	N4574N	D17S-6727	*Dakota Ag Service, Britton, SD
c	N4607N	D17S-6927	*Chad N. Koppie, Gilberts, IL
c	N4612N	D17S-6874	*Charles W. Harley, Davenport, IA
c	N46296	F17D-332	*Richard G. Miller, Brighton, CO
c	N4688N	D17S-6682	*Carl R. King, Williamson, GA
c	N47024	C17B-102	*Christine M. St.Onge, Wexford, PA
c	N4710V	G17S-B-13	*George W. Freeman, Canton, NC
r	N47D	D17R-289	A/C & Engineering Enterprises, Moore, OK
c	N480	D17S-4810	*480 Stag Club Inc., Santa Ynez, CA
c	N48401	E17B-151	John J. Cournoyer, Ellsinor, MO
c	N48974	E17B-191	*James C. Spriggs, Aguila, AZ
c	N49301	F17D-250	*Oley Swanson Poer, Greensboro, NC
r	N49704	F17D-261	*John R. Bowden, Lampasas, TX
r	N499N	17R-1	*Steven K. Pfister, Santa Paula, CA
c	N50256	F17D-258	*E. Perry Miller, Brighton, CO
c	N50650	E17B-143	*Robert A. Kreutzer, San Diego, CA
c	N5074N	D17S-6680	*Lee W. Schaller, Sausalito, CA
r	N50959	D17A-305	*John L. Harbor, Central Point, OR
c	N50A	F17D-271	*Glenn Pray, Broken Arrow, OK
c	N51121	D17S-4914	*Paul B. Supan Jr., Middleton, PA
r	N51152	D17S-137	Phillip K. Ray, Arlington, TX
d	N51746	D17S-4890	Charles F. Nicholls, West Couina, CA
c	N51969	D17S-4898	*Lane C. Leonard, Covina, CA
r	N51MM	D17S-4886	Alonzo Anzaldua, Los Indios, TX
c	N52686	D17S-4882	*Bruce C. Pugsley, Stanford, CA
c	N52931	D17S-4833	*Richard Wixom, Janesville, WI
c	N52962	D17S-6880	*J.E. Swarthout, Tavares, FL
c	N53298	D17S-4900	*Richard L. Perry, Hampshire, IL
c	N5447N	D17S-4875	(Sale reported) Malcolm McGregor, El Paso, TX
c	N54657	D17S-4906	Holman Enterprises, Kalispell, MT
c	N555PC	D17S-6873	*C.W. Dawson, Palm City, FL
r	N5653N	D17S-6766	Robert S. Dedek, Rosenburg, TX
r	N57829	E17B-198	*James H. Bohlander, Marengo, IL
c	N582	D17S-6704	*Heinz G. Peier, Switzerland
r	N58N	D17S-6762	*Richard J. Kasper, Smithtown, NY
r	N59700	F17D-413	Veronica Ann Francis, Saylorsburg, PA
c	N60149	D17S-4867	Bushfield Aircraft Co., Augusta, GA

* = Staggerwing Club member. r = Restoration. d = Display.

c = Current. p = Parts. s = Stored. m = Dismantled.

	Registration	Model	Registered Owner
c	N61278	D17S-4859	*H. Erik Barnes, Kenai, AK
p	N61862	D17S-4877	*Denzell W. Marshall, Pasadena, CA
r	N63477	D17S-6720	*Jack S. Robins, Broomfield, CO
c	N63549	D17S-6729	*Mervyn E. Asher, Las Vegas, NV
c	N65594	D17S-3097	Cary Flyers, Inc., Cary, NC
c	N663	D17S-4903	*Maurice Clavel, Wauchula, FL
c	N66426	D17S-6718	*John L. Harbour, Central Point, OR
c	N67543	D17S-6908	*Thom W. Mayer, Santa Cruz, NM
c	N67550	D17S-6717	*Robert C. Van Ausdell, Santa Paula, CA
c	N67555	D17S-6876	*Commercial Honing Co., Portland, OR
c	N67677	D17S-6724	*Thomas Allen Webb, Riverside, CA
c	N67716	D17S-6733	Troy E. Stimson, Justin, TX
p	N67734	D17S-3093	*George S. York, Mansfield, OH
d	N67735	D17S-6935	*Kermit Weeks, Miami, FL
c	N67736	D17S-4848	W. Spriggs, Santa Paula, CA
p	N67747	D17S-4847	*(Sale reported)*
r	N67769	D17S-146	*George S. York, Mansfield, OH
r	N69217	D17S-3100	*Lloyd W. Pote, Sturbridge, MA
c	N69H	D17S-4896	*John M. Averill, Byromville, GA
c	N700N	G17S-B-19	*John H. Thomson, Carson City, NV
c	N70E	G17S-B-11	*Denzell W. Marshall, Pasadena, CA
c	N7024K	D17S-6870	Joseph Erale, Bay Shore, NY
c	N711JR	D17S-6672	*Layton A. Humphrey, Dallas, TX
c	N711ZZ	D17S-4811	*Rosie O'Grady Orlando, Inc., Orlando, Fl
c	N71E	D17S-6919	Bruce R. Stevenson, White Salmon, WA
r	N722MD	D17S-6750	*(Sale reported)* Roanoke, VA
c	N75544	D17S-3088	Neal A. Richardson, Rancho Palos Verde, CA
p	N75614	D17S-4806	*Victor M. Schmidt, Corbett, OR
r	N75728	D17S-3086	*Larry D. Keitel, Tempe, AZ
c	N79091	D17S-1020	*John T. Henry, Fort Collins, CO
c	N79484	D17S-4917	*Gene E. Moser, Monterey Park, CA
c	N7MB	D17S-6767	*Markley C. Brown, Santa Barbara, CA
c	N80024	D17S-4915	*Connie L. Ashura, Strasburg, CO
r	N800K	B17L-25	Gordon L. Kraft, Palatka, FL
c	N80305	G17S-B-4	*James C. Gorman, Mansfield, OH
c	N80306	G17S-B-5	*Anna W. Freeman, Griffen, GA
r	N80308	G17S-B-7	Clayton J. Carriveau, Franksville, WI
r	N80309	G17S-B-8	*James S. Francis, Westfield Centre, OH
c	N80312	D17S-6886	*Robert J. Welsh, Pasadena, CA

* = Staggerwing Club member. r = Restoration. d = Display.

c = Current. p = Parts. s = Stored. m = Dismantled.

	Registration	Model	Registered Owner
c	N80315	G17S-B-14	*William G. Quinn, Columbia, MO
c	N80316	G17S-B-15	*William W. Halverson, Minneapolis, MN
s	N80317	G17S-B-16	Robert Watkins, Ontario, CA
c	N80321	G17S-B-20	Raymond J. Jones, Stuart, FL
c	N838	D17S-6731	*Richard W. Carr, St. Petersburg, FL
r	N8589A	G17S-B-18	*Jack G. Rouse, Boynton Beach, FL
r	N9003A	G17S-B-2	*Bill White, Boring, OR
c	N911	G17S-B-12	*H.H. Holloway Jr., Baton Rouge, LA
c	N9113H	D17S-4823	Donald R. Quinn, Inver Grove Hts., MN
c	N9115H	D17S-1014	*Beecher Wiggins, Leesburg, IN
r	N91H	E17B-219	Vincent J. Pincetich, Northridge, CA
c	N9169H	D17S-6879	*Joe E. Haynes, Dallas, TX
r	N9290H	D17S-6726	*Steven E. Dyer, Brighton, CO
s	N92TJ	D17S-6918	David L. Fayman, Lawrence, KS
c	N9370H	D17S-4846	*Denzell Marshall, Pasadena, CA
c	N9376H	D17S-1018	William S. Pinette, King Salmon, AK
c	N9405H	D17S-4803	*Rolp Versen, Duisburg, West Germany
r	N9459H	D17S-6700	Roy D. Reagan, Chico, CA
c	N9463H	D17S-6900	*Decherd W. Edmondson, Vinemount, AL
c	N9465H	D17S-6898	*Robert C. Collins, Coronado, CA
c	N9466H	D17S-6688	James R. Almand, Grand Prairie, TX
c	N9470H	D17S-6670	*Donald L. Lee, Newport Beach, CA
c	N9597H	D17S-4840	*Steven J. Zuzow, Dearborn Heights, MI
r	N95MA	D17S-1013	*Thomas Leo Smith, Kent, WA
d	N962W	C17B-100	*Alton E. Cianchette, Newport, ME
c	N9724H	D17S-4807	*Stephen C. Johnson, Sherman, CT
c	N97P	D17S-4837	*Gary Gransfors, Inver Grove Heights, MN
c	N9873H	D17S-4839	*Lee Moyle, Heyburn, ID
c	N9885H	D17S-3091	*Philip Kent Livingston, Anchorage, AK
c	N9886H	D17S-6910	*Beecher Wiggins, Leesburg, IN
c	N9936H	D17S-4808	*Uwanna P. Perras, Redwood City, CA
r	N99384	D17S-?	(Sale reported) (Quoted as 01674)
c	N996	C17R-74	Don M. Robinson, Brownsville, TX
c	N99DV	G17S-B-9	*E. Duke Vincent, Montecito, CA
d	VH-ACU	F17D-248	Joe Drage, Wangaratta, NSW, Australia
d	VH-BBL	D17S-6763	Joe Drage, Wangaratta, NSW, Australia
r	VH-BOU	C17L-107	A.J. Smithwell, Sydney, Australia
c	VH-MJE	D17S-4922	Joe Palmer, Sydney, Australia
c	VH-UXP	C17B-108	Mike Priestly, Aubury, NSW, Australia

---

* = Staggerwing Club member. r = Restoration. d = Display.

c = Current. p = Parts. s = Stored. m = Dismantled.

	Registration	Model	Registered Owner
r	ZS-AJT	D17S-4885	A.J. Torr, Rand, South Africa
p	ZS-BBZ	D17S-6768	South African Air Force Museum, Pretoria
d	(44-76068)	UC-43-6913	*USAF Museum, Wright-Patterson AFB, OH
d	(Bu23688)	GB-2-6700?	USS Yorktown Memorial, Charleston, SC

* = Staggerwing Club member. r = Restoration. d = Display.

c = Current. p = Parts. s = Stored. m = Dismantled.

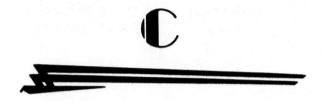

Factory
serial numbers

Military serials for the production of U.S. Navy and U.S. Army Air Corp/Air Forces Beechcraft Model 17s cannot be added together because many military Beechcrafts simultaneously carried at least two U.S. Navy, USAAF, British, and Brazilian Armed Forces numbers. To assess the correct military production, reference must be made to the factory serial number. This indicates a total of 353 prewar Model 17s produced, including 33 aircraft for military air forces. A total of 412 military Model 17s were produced during World War II. Twenty postwar Model G17S were completed, making a grand total of 785 single-engined Beechcrafts built. In addition, 20 Beechcraft Model 17s were license-built in Japan.

Beech Aircraft assigned factory serial numbers in sequence from #1 and up regardless of Model. Note factory #62 is the first twin-engined Model 18. The four-figure factory serials include the wartime production of the single-engined UC-43/GB-2, and twin-engined C-45/JRB, AT-7/SNB, AT-10, and AT-11/SNB.

Beech 17 and Military	Beech 18/C-45, AT-7/AT-10/AT-11
1–61	62
63–168	169 – 178
179–219	220*–224
225–264	265 –269
270–289	290–292
	(293)–294

Beech 17 and Military	Beech 18/C-45, AT-7/AT-10/AT-11
295–314	(315)–316
	(317)–318
	(319–320)
	321
	(322–324)
325–339	340–353
354–363	364–380
	(381–384)
385–424	425–429
	430–1012
1013–1035	1036–3080
3081–3124	(3125–3178)
3179–3205	3206–4790
4791–4940	4941–6668
6669–6768	6769–6868
6869–6936	6937–8700
Total: 765	( ) = not built
	* Rebuilt as #223

Postwar, Beech Aircraft began a factory serial letter-number group, and the Model G17S Staggerwing was in this series, B-1 to B-20.

U.S. Army
Air Corps/Air Force

Three "service test" Model 17s were delivered to the U.S. Army Air Corps:

AC39-139/141   YC-43   #295/297

USAAF Impressments
A total of 118 Beechcraft Model 17s were impressed into the USAAC during WW2. The various models were:

13	D17R	as UC-43A	1	D17A	as UC-43F
13	D17S	as UC-43B	10	C17B	as UC-43G
38	F17D	as UC-43C	3	B17R	as UC-43H
31	E17B	as UC-43D	3	C17L	as UC-43J
5	C17R	as UC-43E	1	D17W	as UC-43K

The listing that follows is in ascending USAAF serial number order, to assist identification of photographs:

AF Serial	Designation	Factory	Registration
42-22246	UC-43C	258	NC290Y
42-36825		250	NC2595
42-38226	UC-43A	214	NC18789
42-38227		215	NC18790
42-38228		313	NC20776
42-38229		289	NC20752
42-38230		405	NC21919
42-38231		167	NC18565
42-38232	UC-43B	146	NC18027
42-38233		396	NC129M

AF Serial	Designation	Factory	Registration
42-38234		199	NC18776
42-38235		186	NC18582
42-38236		416	NC1244
42-38237	UC-43C	391	NC21921
42-38238		333	NC20798
42-38239		275	NC20789
42-38240		394	NC29786
42-38241		310	NC20772
42-38243		393	NC21922
42-38244		312	NC20774
42-38245	UC-43A	278	NC203W
42-38246	UC-43C	242	NC19454
42-38247		390	NC303W
42-38248		276	NC20790
42-38281	UC-43B	422	NC1600
42-28282	UC-43A	166	NC400
42-38283	UC-43C	331	NC19451
42-38284		259	NC289Y
42-38357	UC-43A	148	NC18029
42-38358		180	NC18576
42-38359	UC-43B	362	NC900
42-38361	UC-43C	272	NC238Y
42-38362		241	NC18783
42-38363		273	NC292Y
42-43517		335	NC20754
42-43845	UC-43D	153	NC18042
42-46635	UC-43C	211	NC18786
42-46636	UC-43D	193	NC18559
42-46905	UC-43B	355	NC239Y
42-46906	UC-43C	240	NC18782
42-46907		255	NC18568
42-46908		413	NC21935
42-46909	UC-43D	190	NC18043
42-46910		158	NC18556
42-46914	UC-43C	412	NC21932
42-46915	UC-43D	196	NC18587
42-46916	UC-43C	410	NC248Y
42-47383	UC-43A	218	NC18793
42-47384	UC-43B	415	NC21902
42-47385	UC-43C	243	NC19471
42-47386		389	NC3048
42-47387		277	NC20791

AF Serial	Designation	Factory	Registration
42-47388		281	NC2627
42-47389	UC-43E	82	NC16434
42-47442	UC-43D	156	NC17071
42-47443		191	NC18044
42-47444		142	NC17091
42-47445		162	NC18560
42-47446		189	NC18585
42-47447		138	NC17083
42-47448		145	NC18026
42-47449	UC-43C	337	NC20771
42-47450		256	NC18573
42-49070	UC-43D	151	NC18040
42-49071	UC-43F	305	NC19453
42-52999	UC-43A	72	NC15817
42-53000	UC-43D	212	NC18787
42-53001		192	NC18558
42-53002	UC-43B	287	NC20750
42-53005	UC-43D	208	NC18785
42-53006	UC-43G	143	NC17092
42-53007	UC-43D	197	NC18588
42-53008		411	NC21900
42-53013		251	NC19479
42-53021		155	NC17069
42-53508		141	NC16449
42-53509		207	NC18784
42-53511		231	NC19467
42-53516		159	NC18557
42-53517		205	NC903
42-56085	UC-43B	183	NC18579
42-56087	UC-43D	140	NC17085
42-61092		163	NC2388
42-61093		198	NC18775
42-61097	UC-43B	216	NC18791
42-68337	UC-43C	252	NC19480
42-68339	UC-43A	137	NC17082
42-68340	UC-43B	279	NC20793
42-68359	UC-43D	144	NC18025
42-68360		154	NC17066
42-68855	UC-43G	67	NC15812
42-68856	UC-43H	53	NC15414
42-78019		69	NC15814
42-78039	UC-43E	76	NC15834

AF Serial	Designation	Factory	Registration
42-88620	UC-43G	125	NC17063
42-88628		99	NC16440
42-88629		102	NC16443
42-88634		88	NC15845
42-88636	UC-43C	283	NC2626
42-94124	UC-43D	149	NC18038
42-94133	UC-43J	105	NC16446
42-94137	UC-43H	54	NC15411
42-97048	UC-43C	338	NC294Y
42-97049		261	NC291Y
42-97050		392	NC2801
42-97411		260	NC19469
42-97413	UC-43J	83	NC15813
42-97415	UC-43G	134	NC17079
42-97417	UC-43H	116	NC2000
42-97420	UC-43J	109	NC15836
42-97424	UC-43E	79	NC1600
42-97426	UC-43G	98	NC16439
42-97427		101	NC16442
42-97428		95	NC16436
42-97431	UC-43E	80	NC2166
42-107277	UC-43K	164	NX18562
42-107411	UC-43C	332	NC20797
42-107414		245	NC19473

USAAF Serial Numbers

Production of Beechcraft Model 17s during World War II:

Contract W535-ac-1042 (DA): $19,238.00.

Air Force Serial	Designation	Total
AF42-38665-38691	UC-43-BH*	27
AF43-10818-10892	UC-43-BH	75

Contract AN.31386

Air Force Serial	Designation	Total
AF44-67700-67804	UC-43-BH	105
AF44-76029/76091	UC-43-BH	63

*Suffix letters indicate manufacturer and factory. (BH: Beech, Wichita, Kansas)

U.S. Navy

Eleven prewar production JB-1 and GB-1 aircraft were delivered to the U.S. Navy.

Navy Serial	Designation	Factory	Total
BuNo. 0801	JB-1	115	1
1589/1595	GB-1	298/304	7
1898/1900	GB-1	385/387	3

U.S. Navy Impressments

A total of 11 Beechcraft Model 17 were impressed into the United States Navy during WW2 as GB-1 and GB-2. All were D17S except No. 136, which was a D17W, and No. 30, a F17D.

Navy Serial	Designation	Factory	Registration
BuNo. 09765	GB-2	400	NC20755
09766	GB-1	406	NC240Y
09768	GB-1	421	NC21933
09772	GB-1	401	NC21917
09773	GB-2	407	NC21920
09774	GB-2	398	NC20779
09776	GB-1	136	NC17081
09777	GB-1	165	NC18563
09778	GB-1	168	NC18566
09780	GB-1	185	NC18581
09800	GB-1	30	NC20770

U.S. Navy Serial Numbers

Navy Serial	Designation	Total
BuNo. 0164/01646	GB-2	23

Navy Serial	Designation	Total
12330/12353		47
23657/23756		100
32867/32915	(Ex RN)	49
32992/33066		75
(85391/85485 Cancelled)		(68)

Foreign Air Forces

Marks	Factory	Country	Total
11/11	#9/77	Honduras	2
A39-1,2,3	#248/357/108	Australia	3
*	181/182/217	China	
*	235-237/239		
*	325-326		
*	328-329		11
B-941-S	?	Bolivia	1
BC-1,2	124/6885	Finland	2
Be205-208	358-361	Brazil Navy	4
DR628, DS180,	295/118	Royal Air Force	
EB279/280	?/327		4
FL653/670	*	Royal Air Force	18
FZ428/439	*	Royal Air Force	12
FT461/535	*	Royal Navy	75
FAB01/051	*	Brazil Air Force	51
NZ573	107	New Zealand	1
PB.1	420	Netherlands	1
R319/R329/R343	104/?/161	Argentina	3
S-501	4939	Uruguay	1

*Unknown

G

GI7S checklist and power chart

Before Start

Fuel Selectors	Main Tank
Cowl Flap	Open
Circuit Breakers	In
Parking Brakes	Set
Carb Heat	Cold
Oil Heat	Open
Oil Bypass	Closed
Mixture	Rich
Throttle	Set
Altimeter	FBP
Compass	Slaved
Clock	Set
Battery Master	On
Alternator Field	On
Fuel Quantity	OK

Taxi

Numbers   Set

V Liftoff	70
V Max Grad	95
V Climb	120

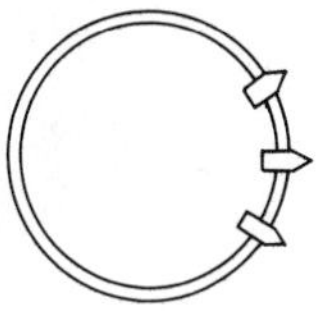

Radios   Set

Takeoff

Controls	Free
Instruments	Normal
Gas	Main
Flaps	Up
Trim	Set
Prop	Flat Pitch
Runup	Mags Checked
Final Items	
Transponder	Code set, on
Lights	Strobe on
Tailwheel	Locked

Takeoff

450 BHP 2300 RPM 50 GPH

FL	−20F	0F	+20F	+40F	+60F	+80F	100F
MSL	34.3	34.9	35.4	36.0	36.5	36.5	36.5
10	34.0	34.6	35.1	35.7	36.2	36.2	36.2
20	33.7	34.3	34.8	35.4	35.9	35.9	
30	33.4	34.0	34.5	35.1	35.6	35.6	
35	33.2	33.8	34.3	34.9	35.4	35.4	

Meto

400 BHP 2200 RPM (100%) 44 GPH

FL	−20F	0F	+20F	+40F	+60F	+80F	100F
10	30.1	30.7	31.2	31.8	32.3	32.7	33.2
20	30.4	31.0	31.5	32.1	32.6	33.0	
30	30.7	31.3	31.8	32.4	32.9	33.3	
40	31.0	31.6	32.1	32.7	33.2	33.5	
50	31.3	31.9	32.4	33.0	33.5	33.8	

Climb

300 BHP 2000 RPM (75%) 28 GPH

FL	−20F	0F	+20F	+40F	+60F	+80F	100F
10	26.8	27.4	27.9	28.5	29.0	29.5	30.0
20	26.5	27.1	27.6	28.2	28.7	29.2	29.7
30	26.2	26.8	27.3	27.9	28.4	28.9	
40	25.9	26.5	27.0	27.6	28.1	28.6	
50	25.7	26.3	26.8	27.4	27.9	28.4	
60	25.4	26.0	26.5	27.1	27.6	28.1	
70	25.1	25.7	26.2	26.8	27.3	27.8	
80	25.5	26.1	26.6	27.2	27.7		
90	25.2	25.8	26.3	26.9	27.4		
100	24.9	25.5	26.0	26.6	27.1		

Cruise

240 BHP 1850 RPM (60%) 20 GPH

FL	−20F	0F	+20F	+40F	+60F	+80F	100F
10	27.1	27.3	27.7	28.0	28.3	28.6	28.9
20	26.7	27.0	27.3	27.6	28.0	28.3	28.6
30	26.4	26.7	27.0	27.3	27.6	27.9	
40	26.1	26.3	26.7	27.0	27.3	27.5	
50	25.7	26.0	26.3	26.6	26.9	27.2	
60	25.4	25.7	26.0	26.3	26.6	26.9	
70	25.0	25.3	25.7	26.0	26.3	26.5	
80	24.7	25.0	25.3	25.6	25.9		
90	24.4	24.7	25.0	25.3	25.6		
100	24.0	24.3	24.6	24.9	25.2		

Approach

Numbers   Set

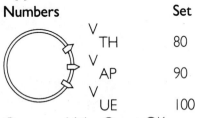

	Set
V_{TH}	80
V_{AP}	90
V_{UE}	100

Gas   Main, Quant OK
Mixture Rich

Landing

Gas	Main
Undercarriage	Down, 3 Green
Mixture	Rich, 90F Carb
Prop	2200 RPM
Final Items	
Tail Wheel	Locked

Touch and Go

Prop	Flat Pitch
Flaps	Up
Carb Heat	Cold
Trim	Set

After Landing

Prop	Flat Pitch
Flaps	Up
Carb Heat	Cold
Transponder	Off
ADF	Off
NAVS	Off

Parking

Prop	High Pitch
Battery Master	Off
Alternator Field	Off
Radio Master	Off
Mixture	ICO
Ignition	Off
Fuel Selectors	Off

Bibliography

Organizations

Beech Aircraft Corp., Wichita, Kansas.
Federal Aviation Administration, Oklahoma City, Oklahoma
Fleet Air Arm Museum, Yeovilton, England.
Royal Air Force Museum, Hendon, England.

Books

Aerospace: Wichita Perspective, John Zimmerman, 1966.
Australia's Military Aircraft, Ross Gillett, 1987.
Beech, William H. McDaniel, 1947.
Beechcraft: Staggerwing to the Starship, E.H. Phillips, Flying Books, 1987.
British Civil Aircraft, Vol.1, A.J. Jackson, 1959.
Challenge of the Poles, John Grierson.
High, Wide and Frightened, Louis Thaden.
Racing Planes Vols. 3, 7, Reed Kinert, 1940, 1971.
Story of Wichita, J.T. Nevill, 1930.
Staggerwing: The Story of the Classic Beechcraft Biplane, Robert T. Smith and Tom Lempicke, Staggerwings Unltd., 1967, 1979.
They Flew the Bendix Race, Don Dwiggins, 1965.
Travel Air: Wings over the Prairie, E.H. Phillips, Flying Books, 1982.
U.S. Marine Corps Aircraft 1914–1959, W.T. Larkins, 1959.
U.S. Navy Aircraft 1921–1941, W.T. Larkins, 1961.
U.S. Civil Aircraft Series, Vol. 9, ATC #801-Emigh "Trojan"—817 Fokker "Friendship," by Joseph Juptner, TAB/Aero, 1982.

Index